# Fit-For-Purpose
# Leadership #5

**LeadershipGigs**

**WRITING MATTERS**

**Fit For Purpose Leadership #5**

First published in July 2019

Writing Matters Publishing (UK)
info@writingmatterspublishing.com
www.writingmatterspublishing.com

ISBN 978-1-912774-27-2 (e-book)
ISBN 978-1-912774-26-5 (pbk)

Editor: Andrew Priestley

Contributors: Mari Williams, David Robson, Teresa Bough, Ben Freedman and Craig Carey, Rebecca Godfrey PhD, Graham Keen, Steven Shove, Mike Hax Hacker, Sophia Giblin, Will Grover, Barbara Khattri, Kim Newman, Stuart Ritchie, Linda Hill, Claire Croft, Diana Barnett, Nicholas Charles, Laura Piccardi, Errol Lawson, Jason Graystone, Andrew Priestley

# Dedication

Dedicated to business leaders everywhere
- and to you - someone who has decided
to positively impact *your* world.

# Contents

# About Leadership Gigs

*Leadership Gigs* is a global online community, for business leaders - CEOs, MDs, executives; SME business owners; and entrepreneurs. It was created in response to the need for confidential, authentic, conversations with like-minded peers.

*Leadership Gigs* works because it allows leaders to connect on line with peers to a broad base of experience from a diverse range of industries ... without the ads.

The glue, of course, is *Trust*.

Importantly, *Leadership Gigs* provides a confidential forum for sharing and discussing ideas, discussing, reflecting and receiving candid, constructive feedback. It allows members to share concerns, doubts, express vulnerability and receive candid and direct support.

Feedback suggests that being able to talk freely with other business leaders reduces stress and isolation and leads to insights, key light bulb moments and breakthroughs.

# Welcome to Fit For Purpose #5

*Fit For Purpose Leadership* asks high performing, business leaders to share their current best thinking on leadership. Initially, we fielded articles on six core leadership categories but now its more of an adventure. We discovered that keeping it open-ended works much better for writers an readers. It's less prescriptive - and this new book now feels more like a journey of discovery.

Essentially, we are still asking our authors to consider questions like:

- Who are the people at the very top of your field?
- What are they like?
- What makes them special?
- What do you think makes a good leader? Or a great leader?
- Who do you admire, respect and who would follow without a second thought?
- What are they doing well that has your attention?
- Who is influencing and shaping the way you want to run your business?
- What does best practice look like?
- What are the emerging leadership trends?
- What looks like game changing, peak performance or high end?
- What else is good for leaders to know?

But these are far more than questions to prompt academic speculation. Right now we need good leadership. For example, right now, it is impossible to ignore political leadership, locally and globally. And it seems everyone has an opinion on what *good* is or isn't.

Subsequently, leadership is really being questioned and scrutinized closely.

Two current trends are *trust* and *alignment.*

In an era of fake news, people are asking, *Who can I trust? Can I trust this? Can I believe you? Can I trust you?*

For example, world governments are embracing climate change initiatives labelling climate change as an emergency. Sir David Attenborough and Dr David Suzuki, both highly-trusted environmentalists, are saying we have good reason to be worried about the planet. But equally impressive members of the scientific community are climate change deniers claiming that the global warming narrative is, in itself, over-heated.

Sure ... but ...

Who do we trust? Who do we believe? Who should we trust? Whose lead do we follow? And how do we then choose to act?

And while we have always asked, *Why should I buy from you?* we are now asking, *What do you stand for?, What are your values?, What side of the argument are you on?* and *What is the right side of the argument?*

Thought leaders like Rebecca and Veronica Mason (experts in social differentiation), Ben Freedman and Craig Carey (social enterprise consultants), Danielle Chiel (a registered B Corp fashion manufacturer), Phillip Priestley (private chef and exponent of ethically farmed/sympathetically sourced), Cathy Burke (global ambassador for *The Hunger Project*) are all reporting that verifiable transparency is the currency of leaders wanting to run values-based corporations.

There is an emerging class of leaders that view ethical performance as standard practice. And leaders that place higher value on empathy, inclusiveness and openness.

In the last three years, we have seen a rapid increase in companies embracing social value and differentiation. That involves challenging choices and decisions.

*Who do you choose to be? How do you define yourself and your company? And how do you behave? Who is the ideal you? And can we even come from that space?*

And what does the new *good* look like in leadership?

This edition embraces topics covering identity, business performance, strategic thinking, operational excellence, high performing teams and excellent communication. But all underpinned by a deeper sense of purposeful leadership.

*Fit For Purpose Leadership 5* has much to challenge and inspire. Enjoy.

# Are You Fit For Leadership?

## Mari Williams

Genuine leaders are different: they're disruptive, risk taking, humble, empathetic and they see the bigger picture. They're not out to gain status symbols; they're out to create world change. They resonate excellence and humility.

True leadership does take a special kind of person and you may not be it – you may be an awesome follower! However, the fact you are reading this book and not one with a title like, *How to lie on a beach and earn millions while you tan* might mean that you are.

If you have any presence on social media, you'll be used to seeing positive affirmations inspiring you to become an expert or leader. *Everyone can lead!* is the claim, yet some people can't lead.

Can you?

Pause. Have you ever stopped to reflect on why you're a leader or aspire to be?

We all *lead* our lives through the decisions we make. I'm passionate that each of us create the change we want to see in ourselves, but when it comes to decisions that affect our human race and planet, I want appropriately skilled people in charge. I've interviewed and worked with hundreds of leaders and aspiring leaders. True leaders stand out, without trying. They exude confidence, experience, creativity, yet they're humble. All mention their mistakes and learnings and always mention the support of others (that's those awesome followers) as being imperative in their successful leadership.

So, which are you?

## Would you hit the button?

Authentic leadership is being able to make decisions that may affect millions of people and knowing in your inner core that the decisions you are making are the best decisions for that moment in time. It's about making the jump from thought to action that most people don't make.

Recently, I saw a hospital which has a button to push if you see someone smoking in the *no smoking* area. A great initiative. But how many will actually take that action and push it? 1%? If that. Most people have a deep sense of worry about what other people think of them; and this blocks their ability to move from thought to action because the thought that others will blame or ridicule them is so humiliating that their brain won't take the risk.

Leaders hit the button.

## Can't not

Martin Luther King said, "I have a dream". Ask a sincere leader and they can articulate their dream within seconds because it's the dream that drives the leadership. In my opinion they can't NOT lead. For those leaders, money, power and labels are unimportant (and yet they may have feelings of desire for those things and be able to rise above that natural emotion). Their driver is to fulfil the dream because the dream is bigger than them.

A genuine leader resides in your community, your schools, your governments, the arts, science, comedy - although they may not be the top person. They exist in the 15-year-old willing to stand at the *United Nations* and fight for the future of our planet. Who do you know who creates change for others? The group that formed to stop houses being built on green belt land? The group that created the club for vulnerable kids? MPs that show their vulnerability because it helps others? Leaders in all fields are instigating change and inspiring millions of awesome followers.

So, what is it that you can't NOT do?

## Who are you?

I have a consulting room full of *leaders*. As a professional, you may feel that *leadership* has become an annoying buzz word. Bookshop shelves groan under the weight of *how to* books.

*These six skills make you a leader* – no they don't. Malcolm Gladwell in *The Tipping Point* highlights different types of people who perform separate functions in society: *if everyone leads, who follows?* A very self-aware man told me, *"I am not a leader, I'm a right-hand man, that's where I excel."*

It's imperative to identify your skill set and own it. When we push everyone in our organisation to lead, we restrict them from discovering their own value.

## Raw ingredients

So, you've worked out your NOT, that thing you can't NOT do. You have the dream. You'd hit the button, so are you ready for leadership? Here's why the answer still might be *no*.

When clients come to me to improve their leadership, they expect a 10-point model to follow. Then I say, we're going to look at your past experiences and your mindset and see how that's stopping you lead. I'm going to explain some neuroscience so you understand why you aren't fulfilling your potential as a leader. By combining this knowledge, we'll transform your unhelpful behaviours and when you've done all this, a model is irrelevant because YOU as a human being, will be fit for leadership. It's a leadership hack: do the work and be successful.

There's no short cut, no hands on your hips reciting your power phrase. An authentic leader deeply knows themselves within their core. They have well-defined thinking and decision-making processes and they see failure as a roundabout not a dead end. They approach life on a slightly different earth axis to the rest of the population. By knowing and trusting themselves, they can recalibrate almost minute-to-minute. How to do this is what I teach my clients.

## Are you brave enough?

The key to this clarity comes from being brave enough to do the personal work so the *WHO you are* becomes clean, in head and heart.

Each day, you work harder to be a better version of yourself. To admit your flaws. You get professional help to guide you. You cannot do this alone if you want to lead well because you will hide from yourself.

You understand that by unblocking your emotional baggage, facing your demons, learning new behaviours and gaining a new mindset – changes come not from theory but from deep within you. You create a clean, clear space in your mind, free of noise, where you see the *truth* in situations and make great decisions.

You have energy that drives you forward when part of you desperately wants to give up. You see the future and all it's potential. You care about humanity and the planet and you care about getting your dream realised. You can't NOT.

Martin Luther King did not set out to give his famous *I have a dream* speech that day, but an awesome follower said, "Tell them about the dream Martin" and changed history. His dream roused the world and generations of awesome followers.

Problems arise when your head is so full of clutter you can't see *your* dream. Like the end of a rainbow, it moves and shifts even though you glimpse its beauty. What if by clearing your blocks you got exact co-ordinates to your desired destination?

## What's your decision?

Born full of hope, wonder and awe, the smallest things thrill us, from our own toes, to the minute world of the creatures that appear when you lift up a rock. Children live in a *land* where everything is, in the true and forgotten meaning of the word: *awesome*. Imagine if you could tune back into that immense curiosity, creativity and action? If you have ever tried to stop a two-year-old, you'll see the force of conviction in play.

But as we grow, life gets in our way, like the rain that stops play, the bully at school, the teacher that criticises you, the boss that doesn't acknowledge how good you are, the promotion you didn't get. It doesn't matter, we ALL have *stuff* that stops us developing our inner selves in pure positivity. That stuff is called LIFE. It's an oblique irony, because that *stuff* often becomes the origin of your dream for change, but you must clear your negative blocks and mind clutter from that stuff so you can harness your power, passion and drive to make the correct decisions needed to truly lead. I have clients who say, "If I clear my negative emotions, I'll lose my drive."

You won't, you'll increase it. All that energy you exert second guessing yourself, worrying what others think, feeling a lack of self-worth (even as another voice tells you: *you are amazing*), is wasted. When you re-right - and I mix that deliberately - this energy is released and it grows your skill set exponentially leaving you with strong self-value, confidence and clarity. Imagine having double or triple the energy that you have now. This allows you to hold in paradox fearing the decisions you make and yet trusting your trained instincts. These and so many other internal resources can be yours.

### Welcome to leadership

My challenge to you is: Are you brave enough or honest enough to clear the blocks that LIFE has put in your way? You begin by creating your best self, then you continue to do the difficult, inspiring, internal work of making sure you are ready for leadership… then you are ready to live your dream…

## About Mari Williams

Mari Williams, *The Mind Architect*. Executive Coach, Conflict Mediator, Cognitive Hypnotherapist, and NLP Practitioner, she is also a Mother of five children. She is currently writing her own book, *The Fulfilled Leader.*

She works with high level talent - CEOs, entrepreneurs and influencers in the arts, science, media and political spaces. They come to her stressed yet successful and wanting to improve their over-thinking, anxiety, relationships and confidence so they can lead well, live well and love well.

She works with structured process which is solution-orientated and dynamic, whilst being human, relatable and authentic. She gets clients unstuck, happy and content. They stop worrying, make better decisions, increase productivity and realise their value and potential in all areas of their lives.

Mari's goal is to enable leaders to find certainty and clarity from within so they create inspirational change in the world.

Mari's values are integrity, professionalism, clarity, equality and world peace!

*mari@mari-williams.com*

*www.mari-williams.com*

*Linkedin: Mari Williams – The Mind Architect*

*Facebook: @williamsthinks*

*Twitter: @williamsthinks*

*Instagram: mariwilliams.mindarchitect*

# Leader Or Leadership?

## David Robson

*Leader* noun: A person or thing that leads.

*Leadership* noun: An act or instance of – leading; guidance; direction

I'm hoping to learn as I'm exploring this with you. So whilst this piece may appear to be wandering at times, that's intentional. At this time I've genuinely come to realise it's important to have a deeper understanding of who and what I am plus how my leadership contribution might improve. I've a starting assumption that I plan to test with you. I believe I can demonstrate leadership, but have not really considered myself a leader. Is it a time in my life to alter that?

*"To everything there's a season and a time to every purpose under the heaven. A time to plant, a time to reap, A time to kill, a time to heal."*

Ecclesiastes

Let's work with the concept of leaders and leadership in a business context; perhaps borrowing from military, politics and elsewhere from time to time.

A few questions to set the scene.

Is it possible to learn how to be a *leader*? Coincidently, I recently saw a tutorial entitled *How to be a Great Leader* – it was a whole six minutes long! In workshops that I lead, you'd often hear me saying *doing is learning* and increasingly I'm doing my level best to learn.

There's two words from ancient Greek associated with knowledge: *logos* and *gnosis*. I invite you to do your own study and reflection on these two. However, there are several metaphors that spring to my own mind.

Again, one that I use goes something like this. Take a large technical manual describing in really great detail how to maintain a car - engine, transmission, suspension, electrical etc. Study it all day long, every day, for a few months. I could sit you down and *test* you on your knowledge and you'd probably do pretty well. However, if I took the manual away from you and simply said, "Go fix that car outside", would you do as well? For me the former scenario demonstrates *logos*; and the latter *gnosis*.

I was once asked, "Quick! - what are three qualities of leadership?" Without really thinking I spat out:

- Vision
- Communication
- Courage

I now think somewhat differently, that the first two are indeed leadership qualities. I now lean towards the third being a demonstration of what's required of a leader. So my current premise is this. You can know about leadership, you can perform acts of leadership, you can only be a leader.

David Goggins advises us to know who you are. This is sound advice from the man you can't hurt. In my world of business turnarounds, I need to be ready to shift roles.

Instigating, negotiating, motivating, conciliating, critiquing and then holding to account – especially myself. If I'm not doing the right thing at the right time, I'm compromised in doing what's needed.

I've had the good fortune to stand in the temple at Delphi, where we are taught that Pythia (the oracle) once profoundly said *Know thyself*. I've contemplated this many times. To me this phrase demonstrates *logos*. Another way it might have actually been phrased, *Know thy self* to me demonstrates *gnosis*.

So why is that important? Let's have some more questions. Is a leader always good at leadership? Is leadership a continuum or a constant? Are there common-core attributes? Can leadership actually be a collective noun?

For the last few years, I've also been helping to re-engineer local government so that it becomes more self-sufficient. And I've learned several more things in connection with our exploration.

Firstly, it might be worth outlining some parameters for you. The smallest Councils operate with income-expenditure budgets around £20-£35 million. Some of the largest around £300 million - £2.75 billion. They engage with individual citizens and, most interestingly, with many tens of thousands of local businesses – of all sizes.

They officially have two categories of leaders – *executive leaders* and *political leaders*. During this work I've found that there's a potential third definition for us to consider. *Leader* noun: someone holding that position. Perhaps I'll return to that another time.

So I've supported organisations of various sizes; from owner-driver start ups, to mid-market public companies, to complex ones employing many thousands. There's another story about the parallels between the human organism and the organisational one – perhaps for another time, as well.

I've found that most people prefer safety and certainty. Leaders too, but they cope continually with uncertainty and they understand that they risk failing. They're human and probably do get scared, but see the job that needs doing right now – and maybe the learning opportunities. Applying leadership they can generate a sense of certainty for others.

In my experience, once you have more than a three or four colleagues you'll need to demonstrate leadership in order to be their leader. Many business founders are great at precisely that, starters rather than leaders. Can you be a leader and not be great at leadership? Or demonstrate leadership yet fail as a leader? Is there a third role as leader-mentors?

Wise founders, who know who they are, will sometimes find an experienced and proven leader to scale their business. Then watch, learn and grow; waiting for the right season. When *fixing* businesses I try to do so on the basis of management apprentices rather than management education. Incidentally I get *free* training with this methodology – provided I'm prepared to get stuck in with them!

Here's some illustrations of people that, to me, seem to demonstrate what I'm feebly attempting to say.

Larry Page co-founded *Google* but recognised he was not the leader needed to scale it to become the global phenomenon it is today and handed the reins to Eric Schmidt. Larry is now heading *Google* and Eric is Chairman of *Alphabet,* the holding company.

Steve Jobs led *Apple* - from his garage to *Apple Campus,* Cupertino. Then things went wrong, he too decided to recruit someone who could scale – and it all went wrong. His choice was flawed and he didn't truly step aside.

Jack Welch was a leader when his character was needed by *General Electric* famously losing the bottom 10% performing managers each year. However his leadership became questionable when markets changed.

Richard Branson seems to have an intuitive grasp of business and has a unique leadership style, without necessarily giving the appearance of a great leader.

Winston Churchill was a leader when we needed one most. But maybe his prior and post leadership qualities could have stood some improvement, perhaps.

Theresa May probably failed on both counts. At first when a leader was needed; and subsequently when leadership was tested.

Anyway, I've actually enjoyed this short stroll with you - but got to go. So, I'll leave you with a few very personal things I've learned; both getting here and during these paragraphs.

Think critically, act diligently, be courageous, be always aware of the rewards of *gnosis* via your actions. Be straight with yourself. Always give your best leadership contribution and you stand a chance of being a leader – when it's needed.

## About David Robson

David studied his MBA at *Manchester Business School.* Then agency marketing; mainly large organisations, *Ford Motor Company, Littlewoods Group, MetroMedia U.S.* etc. General management in telecoms, media, technology in UK, USA, Europe and East negotiating innovative Joint Ventures.

He's built, bought and turned around companies – early stage to stock market. David's success in business turnarounds led to a structured methodology, also re-purposed for Public Sector.

David has invested in early stage or under-performing companies. Transforming business models and management - increasing profits and value. He's worked with investment companies including Angel, VC and Private Equity.

These models and tools were adapted for Local Government. His company works with many organisations on asset discovery, leverage, income generation, enterprise and productivity.

This work largely focuses on commercialism and income generation. Alongside enterprise strategies and models, *Archemys* invests in support of Government commercial ventures.

David leads Senior Management and Politicians workshops to shift perspective and mindset - essential as the foundation of transformation strategies.

*www.archemys.com*

*https://linkedin.com/in/davidrobsonarchemys*

# Allies, Ambassadors And Advocates - How Men Are Helping Build An Inclusive Workplace Culture

## Teresa Boughey

'It's just jobs for the girls' and 'They want it all' are just a few of the comments I've heard from male senior leaders when their female colleagues have been appointed into a senior leadership role. The truth is that for some, but not all, these views are sadly their perception of reality.

In addition, I sense the swell of frustration building amongst some executives who question why there's even a need to be talking about gender, let alone explore any of the other protected characteristics such as disability, race, age and sexual orientation, and why the view of the boardroom needs to change. I've also heard male senior leaders state that addressing gaps in pay and seeking to achieve gender disparity in the boardroom isn't required and will in some way mean fewer opportunities for others.

Well let me tell you, creating a workplace which is more diverse, which is inclusive, and which has greater representation of minority groups isn't about less – it's about more. More diverse thinking, more innovation and greater access to a wider talent pool.

However, there's still a long way to go to bring about change.

Whilst government initiatives and legislation might be helping eliminate discrimination and encourage fair pay in the
workplace, the fact remains that it's still a man's world. It's no
one's fault, but if we want to keep the momentum going, we
need to be far more inclusive. We need to create environments
where men don't feel they are being blamed for the workplace
culture, which thankfully is evolving. We need to include them
in the debate, open dialogue and bring them along on the
journey – equally, they must want to.

I truly believe that if we are all to aspire to an inclusive
workplace culture then men need to play their part. What
I mean by this is that we need to include men in the debate,
and we need to make them feel that it is their place to speak
up about diversity and inclusion. That it's OK if you inadver-
tently say the wrong thing without fear of retribution and open
criticism. If the intention is pure, then seek to understand
the right way in which comments and view should be made.
It's important that nothing gets in the way of pushing for
change, as we remove the barriers, we need far more male
allies, ambassadors and advocates.

But what are *allies, ambassadors* and *advocates*, and what do
they do?

This was a question I posed recently when delivering a
keynote speech to an audience of around 60 men (and the
office dog!). I wanted some audience participation and
therefore tasked them to work in pairs and share one example
of when they had acted as an ally, advocate or ambassador for
someone different them.

At first, the question seemed to challenge them, the room
stayed silent for a while and eventually after a period of
reflection the conversations started to flow. I then invited
several members of the audience to share their experience of
when they had been an ally.

Peter recounted a time when he had observed one of

his female colleagues being on the receiving end of an unreasonably demanding boss during a monthly meeting. Peter reflected that he felt uncomfortable as he watched his highly talented colleague being humiliated. He described that this was his boss's *normal* style but was aware of the impact this was having on his colleague. Consequently, he spoke to his boss afterwards, he described how uncomfortable he had felt during the meeting and went on to express his concern about the impact this was having on his colleague.

Richard commented that he was chairing a speaker panel at a management conference. There were four speakers of which one was a woman. During the interview session, Richard noticed that one of the speakers would talk over the women speaker. Richard described how he had appropriately intervened and reminded the panel of speaker etiquette.

Hassan shared how, within his religious community, it was culturally expected that young men would take up professional roles and young women would be involved in arranged marriages and take on a domestic role. Hassan described how he spearheaded a *meet the family* initiative within the company, whereby he would talk to the families, over dinner, about the great career opportunities available to their daughters and described the support and education they would receive. This initiative was incredibly well received and as a result, the company increased its intake of female graduates.

Ian shared the experience of a workshop he had attended when working for a previous organisation which was a heavily male-dominated environment. During an off-site leadership programme, the delegates were encouraged to really tune into who they are and consider the challenges (personal or professional) that they're facing. For many, this felt uncomfortable and many became incredibly emotional as they shared their hopes, fears and aspirations. Ian described how the safe learning environment had enabled them to talk openly in a way that ordinarily they would never feel comfortable to do so. Ian shared that attendees unanimously felt it was an invaluable experience and committed that they would make time to keep the dialogue going once they returned to work.

We can all by allies and ambassadors for each other, but if we are to accelerate the pace of change, then we need more men to step forward (because it is still a man's business world), to be catalysts for change and support and improve the outcomes for everyone, including those in a minority within the workplace.

Here are a few things you can do to LEAD:

## Look and Listen

- Take notice of the workplace environment and observe the employee demographics.
- Consider if management structures are varied and/or balanced. If not be curious about what this means? Ask what talent plans are in place and consider the role you play in identifying talent for the future?
- Be present – listen, show interest in others.

## Educate

- Proactively seek to understand different perspectives and use this as an opportunity to expand your knowledge about the unique differences that people bring to roles.
- Become a mentor – take the opportunity to share your knowledge, to guide someone else to greatness.
- Think about the legacy that you want to leave – what do you want to be known for? What difference do you want to have made for others?

## Action

- When chairing a meeting attune to behaviours in the room – are there one or two people who domineer the discussions? Does everyone have an equal voice and/or opportunity to contribute?
- Stand up and confront unacceptable behaviour. Great responsibility comes with being a leader and others will look to you for guidance and judge your behaviour as a role model. You need to ensure that your behaviours are congruent with that of an ambassador.

## Determination

- Ambassadors and allies will listen to others and enable advancements.
- To actively enable the advancement of others, you should identify opportunities for development. This could be a small thing, such as chairing the next team meeting, or something larger like leading on a key project.
- Encourage your colleagues to take their full entitlement to such benefits as 'family-friendly working arrangements and/or flexible working.

If we are to achieve a transformation in our workplaces, then we need to do so in unison. Our societal needs will continue to evolve and it's important to keep up the momentum. The impetus, however, should be about the inclusion of all, as opposed to the exclusion of others. No one should be standing on the side-lines waiting and watching for others to make the change. Everyone needs to play their part otherwise progress will never be made.

The demographics of our senior management teams and boardrooms need to shift so that they become more diverse and reflective of modern day society. Not just in relation to gender, which the government has set voluntary targets against, but also in terms of other protected characteristics such as race, faith, disability and sexual orientation.

If companies want to get ahead of their competitors and attract the best talent in the future, they need to become more representative of the customer base they serve and embrace the positive benefits that a truly diverse organisation can bring.

For the sake of this and future generations I urge you to become an *Ally, Ambassador* or *Advocate* but above all, in the words of Mahatma Gandhi, I urge you to *'Be the change you want to see in the world.'*

## About Teresa Boughey

Teresa Boughey is a Fellow of the CIPD and has over 25 years of strategic HR experience. She works with Executive Boards and Leadership Teams during-times of change and business transformation and is passionate about enabling organisations to create inclusive workplace cultures.

Teresa has grown her business to become one of the top Strategic HR Consultancy practices in the UK, winning several awards. Her achievements include leading on the acquisition of the iconic *Gleneagles Hotel,* delivering business transformations across Europe achieving cost savings of c.€1.5m as well as providing Executive Coaching to Board and C-suite members.

Teresa is a *UK Female Entrepreneur Ambassador* and a member of the *Women and Enterprise* and *Women and Work APPG.*

Learn more at:

*Facebook - https://www.facebook.com/JungleHRLtd/*

*Twitter- @junglejayne21*

*LinkedIn - https://www.linkedin.com/in/teresa-boughey-jungle-hr/*

*Jungle HR website - https://www.junglehr.com*

*Jungle Diversity website - https://www.junglediversity.com*

# Why Employee Engagement Is Key To An Effective Talent Strategy

### Ben Freeman and Craig Carey

In the 20+ years we have been working with leaders in the Social Enterprise Sector, it has become clear that without exception they have been driven to make a sustainable social impact. Just to be clear before we start, as there are many different definitions of what a Social Enterprise is – for us – it's an organisation that has a social purpose at the heart of everything it does. But it also has a core secondary aim to create profit to reinvest to further that purpose.

Social Enterprises come in all shapes and guises across the UK economy – B Corps, Coops, Mutuals, Enterprising Charities, Community Interest Companies totalling approximately 100,000 organisations.

So, what stops them from achieving their goals?

We consistently hear three connected problems:

- **Confused Leadership** – a lack of clarity around purpose, vision, values and market position.
- **Confused Strategy** - around the plans for marketing, sales, finance, operations and talent needed to achieve success.
- **Confused Culture** – a lack of the clear enterprise mindset and behaviour essential to achieve and sustain scale.

For the purposes of this piece we will be focusing on the strategy that rules over all - *Talent*.

Money is great. It buys time, it buys equipment, it buys advertising to drive sales but while all of these are important, the reality is that no matter how much money you have if you don't have the right talent, failure is inevitable. It is a bit like putting someone without a license in a Formula 1 car and expecting them not to crash!

Getting the right people in the right place, at the right time - doing the right things, the right way - is the engine that drives everything.

- They give you time. The time to think about clear leadership, the time to focus on what you are good at and the time to create the balance in your life that is so essential to sanity.
- The time to work *on* the business rather than *in* it.
- They also perversely give you money. Through better ideas and through better execution. Better ideas on how to do things not just to generate more income but also to spend less time and resource doing so.
- The right people in the right place at the right time will not only have the clearest understanding of the needs of the customer but also how to fulfil them in the most resource-efficient way.

In our piece, we will give you our brief thoughts on the aim of *Talent Strategy*, explain the key to its effective implementation and finally provide a simple exercise that offers a stark reminder of the cost of getting it wrong!

### What is the purpose of Talent Strategy?

In the world of entertainment, the *talent* are the people who appear up on stage. Everyone else in the business works to promote, project manage and protect those talented, creative people. So, using the word *talent* to describe the people who work in your social enterprise might seem a bit of a stretch.

But it's not. Because, ultimately, however good and useful the idea at the heart of your purpose, vision, values may be, it's the qualities – the talents – of the people working with you that determines the outcome. It's the talent that delivers – or not.

And, because it's so vital to your success, it makes it imperative to have a well thought through *Talent Strategy* – an overall plan for the recruitment, development and retention of the right people, in the right jobs, doing the right things – so that your organisation can deliver the very best results for your customers.

**Exercise One**

Consider your current strategy and give yourself a mark out of ten for how well you feel it deals with the recruitment, development and retention of talent.

Now consider two things you could do in each area that might increase that mark by two.

*"If you can't measure it you can't improve it."*

Peter Drucker

**Why measuring Employee Engagement is key to a successful Talent Strategy?**

For many organisations' talent is often far and away their biggest overhead yet it is common to find no agreed measure of what amounts to success when it comes to the implementation of any strategy.

Rough measures such as wages as a percentage of turnover and overall staff turnover are useful but can also be dangerous without the proper context.

Investing in a robust process of measuring what is commonly called *Employee Engagement* provides that context.

Poor levels can manifest itself in all sorts of ways from high sickness and absenteeism, accidents, shrinkage and overall poor quality of outputs/outcomes that can all too easily get hidden within a set of financial figures.

An effective measure of employee engagement provides a leader with a compass to lead and develop talent strategy.

Done well, it offers an early warning system of potential problems, but it also offers the opportunity to collect and build on the collective intelligence of the whole organisation and maximise the value from it.

## Five tips for running an effective Employee Engagement survey?

- **Create a dialogue not an event** – Annual surveys produce a long list of issues that take time to sift and prioritise and it simply isn't possible to address them all. By carrying out the survey every ninety days it is possible to create more of a dialogue to manage expectations by addressing a few things at a time.

- **Use the same questions and process** – This gives you a clear way of measuring progress. The *Gallup's Q12* survey offers a good place to start as they cover the key areas - see this link for further information *https://q12.gallup.com/public/en-us/Features*

- **Make it easy to complete** – something that people can do in 10-15 minutes.

- **Make it easy to report and respond** – Just as in dialogue there is value in understanding first supported by a clear, timely response. To do this you need a process that provides a clear response quickly and doesn't require hours of collation and reporting.

- **Make it anonymous** – It can take time to win the trust of employees so the ability to make the responses anonymous and indeed if possible, the dialogue anonymous, will lead to produce a more effective dialogue.

## But what if we can't afford it?

Can you afford *not* to do?

Almost everyone we come across has made at least one terrible talent decision in their career yet it's rare for anyone to offer a measure of their failure.

For example, *Harvard Business School* points out that 80% of employee turnover is the result of bad hiring decisions.

## What are the costs of poor talent decisions?

So how much does this cost?

*Oxford Economics* in a 2014 detailed study across five key sectors (IT/tech, accounting, legal, media/advertising and retail) calculated that the loss of an employee earning an annual salary of £25,000 has an average financial impact of £30,614, ranging from £20,113 for retailers to £39,887 for legal firms. These costs take into account the impact of lost output while a replacement gets up to optimal productivity as well as the impact of recruiting and absorbing a new worker. (The cost of the brain drain (2014) – available at *www.oxfordeconomics. com*)

*The Recruitment & Employment Federation* (*www.rec.uk.com*) and Indeed (a leading UK job search engine *www.indeed.co.uk*) on the other hand published a study in June 2017 where they calculated that a poor hire at a middle management level salary of £43,000 could end up costing a business up to £132,015.

# How did the REC these costs breakdown?

| Factors to Consider | Details | Cost Calculation | Cost to You |
|---|---|---|---|
| Wasted Salary | Time the person has been with you | % of average annual earnings | |
| Increased sickness/ absence | Over the average | % of average annual earnings | |
| Professional Fees | Both in terms of the settlement and potentially crisis management | Lawyers' Fees Cost of Employment Tribunal | |
| Compensation/ salary settlement | This cost is higher the more senior the position | £ agreed | |
| Training | Wasted | Specific to the person or share of the annual cost | |
| Replacement Cost | Internal Time & external costs spent on new recruitment process as well as new training Reduced productivity until new recruit reaches optimal productivity (average 28 weeks) | • Advertising costs<br>• Agency Fees<br>• % of annual earnings of hiring managers and interviewers<br>• Induction and training costs<br>• % of annual earnings of new recruit<br>• Cost of any interim<br>• Cost of co-workers and supervisors while they are getting up to speed | |

| Loss of business | Costs associated with missed opportunities not just while working but until the new hire is up to speed | Calculate the total revenue by the number of employees and then the number of weeks |
|---|---|---|
| Fraud | Theft, embezzlement and other fraudulent activities | • Financial loss<br>• Legal Fees<br>• Damaged reputation |
| Impact on staff morale | From seeing how a colleague behaves and is treated | • Lost productivity<br>• Increased staff turnover |
| Impact on reputation and branding | That affects both existing and prospective clients | Time spent managing this<br>Professional fees getting help |

## Exercise Two

As an exercise think of an occasion when you have ended up with the wrong person in the wrong place at the wrong time, doing the wrong things, the wrong way, and allocate a cost under as many of the headings set out in the above table as you believe relevant.

Then calculate your staff turnover last year.

Now multiply 80% of this figure by your average salary.

How do these two figures make you feel?

## Summary

In summary the most important strategy when running a Social Enterprise (or indeed any Enterprise!) is *Talent*.

The plans the leader has for the recruitment, development and retention of the right people, in the right jobs, doing the right things. The key to doing this successfully is to find an effective way of measuring success and we believe that starts with *Employee Engagement*. It will cost money to do well but will in all probability offer an excellent return on investment once you factor in the savings on hiring mistakes.

What are you waiting for?

## About Ben Freedman and Craig Carey

Ben Freedman and Craig Carey set up *Bubble Chamber CIC* in 2014. The purpose is to help leaders of Social Enterprises gain the clarity and courage they need to grow their social impact.

Ben Freedman helped found two national charities, *Aspire,* the UK's leading *Spinal Injuries Charity* and *Breakthrough Breast Cancer,* now the UK's largest *Breast Cancer Charity* and was a founding participant member of *Pilotlight.* He is also the owner of the *Prince Charles Cinema* in Central London as well as *Singalonga Productions* that produces film and theatre events worldwide.

Craig Carey has 20+ years' experience working as a business coach, consultant, non-exec and advisor across a range of different sectors – charity, social enterprise, NGO, SME and finance (specialising in Insolvency and business turnaround) Craig has previously worked at *Social Enterprise UK* and *Pilotlight.* Craig has an MBA and degree in Economics and is an accredited practitioner for *Strategy On A Page, Harrison Assessments* and *Talent Dynamics.*

*www.bubblechamber.net*

*https://www.linkedin.com/in/craig-carey-5103b11a/*

# Vaccinate Your Leaders, Secure The Future Of Your Teams
## How developing a holistic approach to team leadership can future-proof teams in highly regulated industries

### Rebecca Godfrey PhD

In highly regulated industries we often put a lot of effort and focus on developing the right culture, the right structure, the right processes, the right people when we're trying to solve a problem that exists or when we're trying to fix an organisation that just isn't working. But how about if we turn this on its head and instead instil this holistic mindset in all leaders across organisations from the start?

We are driven by innovation and the desire to progress scientifically or technologically to bring much needed, often life changing, solutions to the customers we serve. At the same time, we need to maintain strict compliance with often complex and ever-changing regulations. As a result, our organisations and teams are often shaped organically due to scientific or technological development or in response to regulation change. To be able to flex and adapt within this highly reactive environment, our teams require strong, focused and resilient leadership. For this reason, not only is selection of the most technically talented individuals for leadership positions important, but also developing a holistic leadership mindset in these leaders is vital.

Developing leaders is important for any business, not only for the benefit of the teams they lead and the businesses to whom their talent is invaluable but also for the leaders themselves. Often in our industries many of the attributes for which we were hired at the early stages of our career - analytical, detail-oriented, precise - are somewhat contrary to those we need in leadership - vision, flexibility, creativity. Therefore, leadership development in our industries is an area that requires specific investment not only financially but also in terms of time - time to learn and time to develop key skills and behaviours.

Just as a vaccine arms the body with immunity without exposing it to disease symptoms, we must arm our leaders with clarity, certainty and confidence in their role, allowing them to develop engaged and inspired teams who are empowered and enabled to flex and innovate in the face of change.

### So, how can we develop this holistic leadership mindset?

As a foundation, leaders must have a clear view on their strengths and have an appreciation of their blind-spots. By valuing our strengths, understanding our weaknesses and, as a result, being more self-aware of our own personality preferences, it allows us to be more mindful of how we communicate, make decisions, react to stress and how we manage our teams. Developing empathy and a better understanding of how others may view and interact with the world differently to us, allows us to recognise other's potentially opposing personality preferences and how we may sometimes act, or indeed react, in ways that do not serve our colleagues well.

Building upon this foundation of self-awareness and empathy, we then move to what we term the *5 pillars of team excellence* which together ensure a truly holistic approach to team leadership.

To achieve team excellence leaders must:

- **Advocate for the right culture within their team that's aligned to that of the organisation.** Setting direction and fostering trust through the development of a team purpose, vision for the future and shared team values. When this is done right, you see teams that know who they are, where they are going and how they are going to get there together.

  Involving team members in the development of the team's purpose, vision and values not only brings together insights from the whole team but also allows for important discussions which enhance a sense of belonging, provide an opportunity to discuss any misalignment in values within the team and strengthen commitment to the team and its goals.
  This is not only important for the team but also serves to better communicate this to other stakeholders across and outside of the organisation.

- **Clarify the scope and boundaries of their team's responsibilities and activities.** Ensuring seamless links with interfacing organisations and teams, thereby removing gaps and/or duplication in cross functional projects and processes. In our industries, there often are roles and responsibilities within a process that span teams, departments, offices and in some cases organisations. Therefore, it is vital to ensure that there is clarity as to where the lines are drawn so that each party is clear on their accountabilities and responsibilities.

  At its best any lack of clarity in this regard can result in delays, undue stress and confusion, at its worst we see gaps appearing leading to non-compliance or overlap wasting much needed resources. Reviewing all of the team's activities to ensure that all are clear on what the team is and, perhaps even more importantly, is not responsible for allows us to identify areas where re-negotiation of the boundary lines may be needed. Such negotiations may then take place with interfacing teams and organisations to clarify or to delegate activities that may be better served by those outside of the team due to resource or skill needs.

- **Create the right organisational structure.** Not only in terms of the organisation chart itself but in mindset - removing hierarchical constraints and ensuring empowerment of all team members.

  Establishing subject matter expertise and accountability at all levels within the team. For much of the 20th century, there was a place and value in hierarchy, in a command and control approach in the workplace. Managers outlined and enforced detailed processes and policies for team members to follow which ensured efficiency and reproducibility, something of a necessity in factory work following the industrial revolution.

  Not only today has the work we do and the way in which we do it changed, requiring leaders to enable and empower all team members to be more proactive, accountable and innovative to solve important business challenges and adapt to change, but where we do it has also changed. It is now common place in our industries for team members and their managers to be located in different offices, even different countries. Therefore, now more than ever there is need for personal accountability, trust and partnership with our team members over conformity and intense supervision.

- **Inspire and activate their team with excellent staff development opportunities** so that the individuals within the team have not only the skills, but also the confidence to continuously improve themselves, their processes and their outputs.

  Leaders have a duty of care for their team, for guiding, supporting and developing their team to fulfil their true potential. This is not simply a case of holding a monthly one-to-one meeting and the standard training plan. To really develop the individual, the leader must have an in depth understanding of where they are in terms of both their skill and confidence in their work as only then can they really establish an appropriate development plan and development goals.

  In addition to training of skills, leaders must provide a safe space for discussion, debate, testing, challenge and for failure and must flex their leadership style to the needs of each individual to support their ongoing growth – stepping back or forward as needed.

- **Enable their teams to develop robust, efficient and future proofed end-to-end processes** with enhanced oversight where issues and risks are identified early, mitigated proactively and lead to robust improvements.

Once the first four pillars are established - team members are committed to the vision and aims for the team, clear on the remit of their role, empowered to make important decisions to progress and have been developed both in terms of their skill and confidence, it is they who implement the fifth pillar as you then see them lead the way in developing their processes NOT the leaders.

When non-compliance occurs we so often focus on the process, when it is rarely the process which caused the issue.

An issue within a process is often the symptom but not the cause of the problem.  For the true root cause, one must look across all of the pillars as even when just one of these pillars is missing we see disengagement, inefficiency and the potential for non-compliance.

When the first four pillars are fully established, we have confident subject matter experts in place ready to not only develop, maintain and manage their process but also ready to adjust, update and re-design as the need arises.

## So, how do we use this approach to future proof our teams?

Once in this holistic mindset, rather than only focusing performance reviews on individuals, leaders may then execute periodic reviews on the five pillars - on their team's *Culture, Scope, Structure, Staff* and *Processes*.

Such reviews ensure continuous development and improvement in all areas following scientific, technological and/or regulatory advancement thereby avoiding the need to perform expensive and disruptive organisation overhauls following unchecked scope or structural creep.

We've all heard the phrase *continuous improvement*, this approach is a practical way of implementing this as a mindset and embedding in all teams across the organisation.

## About Rebecca Godfrey PhD

Rebecca is a scientist by background with a PhD in Immunology from the University of Cambridge.

Since leaving academic research, Rebecca's career has given her the opportunity to build and develop a successful drug safety consultancy business, work with and lead colleagues from more than 90 countries, live and work abroad and lead organisations and groups in roles ranging from Company Director of a small consultancy to Global Head and Global Director roles in two of the world's Top 10 Pharma companies.

Having thoroughly enjoyed a successful corporate career, so far, in 2018, Rebecca took the leap to set up *Etheo Limited* bringing her wealth of business experience, outstanding leadership skills, strategy and process development expertise and passion for meeting new challenges to support individuals and leaders build cohesive, high performing teams with a focus on operational excellence.

*Website www.etheo.limited*

*LinkedIn rebecca-godfrey-etheo*

*Facebook rebecca.godfrey.etheo*

*Instagram rebecca.godfrey.etheo*

# Corporate Ethos, EBITDA
# And Leadership Resilience

## Graham Keen

It's common for enlightened business leaders to feel that they must choose between the apparently conflicting goals of maximising profitability and showing kindness and respect for those they lead. In fact, the evidence is overwhelming that treating people well actually optimises financial performance.

It is easy to think that maintaining a primary focus on caring for the well-being of employees is a distraction from the whole-hearted pursuit of superior financial performance. Or even that such soft niceties are an optional nice-to-have that risk allowing people to waste time and effort on non-value adding activities. After all, we are tempted to ask, if we are to achieve the highest possible levels of achievement surely it is axiomatic that every ounce of effort must be applied to that end?

The fallacy in such thinking is probably obvious to you and is this. Maximising an organisational population's efforts towards goals depends on every individual within that population choosing to contribute their own personal maximum exertions. Such discretionary effort cannot be demanded, exhorted or extorted from people with any hope of success.

By definition discretionary effort is volunteered in response to an individual's internal motivations not the extrinsic motivational attempts of others. The leadership task we are faced with then comes down to creating an atmosphere where colleagues choose to contribute optimal discretionary effort. People do that only when they feel a deep emotional engagement with their organisation, its leadership, and their immediate bosses.

We're going to consider together how best to achieve that.

In fact it is relatively straightforward to engage the efforts of intermediate leaders towards ambitious profit targets. However, history teaches us it's more challenging to engineer a culture where those managers, and their reports in turn, pursue financial growth in the people-valuing way required to maintain engagement and discretionary effort amongst colleagues.

Manifesting such values consistently and resiliently under pressure can require widespread positive changes in mindset and behaviour to deliver leadership resilience. Despite many corporate leader's experience that change is elusive, patchy and short-lived, psychology has moved on spectacularly in recent years and our ability to create lasting positive change has been transformed. Through new approaches it is now possible to simultaneously achieve enlightened human values, resilient engagement, and stretching EBITDA goals.

Leadership resilience is about more than eating pressure for breakfast! It's about keeping it together when stuff hits the fan and is the leadership challenge I hear most about:

- from subordinates who are feeling aggrieved at the high handed, callous or self-interested behaviour of their boss
- from managers who are frustrated by their lack of ability to consistently treat people well when things get intense and they feel under pressure
- from chief executives who are puzzled by poor engagement

stats despite the company values being about respect, inclusion, and valuing others.

Happily, there's a lot that can be done.

The lack of behavioural and/or emotional stability, often inaccurately labelled as reverting to type, stems from flawed behavioural change strategies.

Surprisingly, leadership resilience is in fact largely a learned behaviour, not simply genetic, so it can be corrected by people themselves if addressed properly.

However, willpower isn't the answer, and not knowing that fact is a major obstacle to leaders mastering these issues. Using willpower to hold it together under pressure is always going to fail if your unconscious mind is programmed to get autocratic when stressed. And according to the research it seems that most of us are (see following).

Willpower can only override our default responses to situations if we have enough mental bandwidth available, and even then only briefly, and never in extreme cases. The issue is that quite low levels of pressure can consume all our mental bandwidth. In that case our default traits manifest, and for most of us that means getting dissonant (i.e. impacting others' emotional states negatively).

We all know the feeling – when caught between a deadline and a report who is frustrating us, our courtesy and respect can soon wear thin. Importantly however, the costs of such lapses into dissonance are huge:

- Engagement is damaged or destroyed as reports withdraw their follower-ship
- Discretionary effort is withheld, and productivity falls sharply
- Costs rise and/or revenue slows and/or growth falls off
- People vote with their feet – good people don't tolerate leadership dissonance for long.

And most tellingly in leadership terms, behaving resonantly 97% of the time is worthless if 3% of the time a person behaves dissonantly. Two reasons for this:

1. Their reports are never sure which version of their boss turned up today

2. Negative events have a much more powerful effect on people than positive ones:

   a) We are genetically programmed to look for and focus on negative events (it's a survival trait selected in by evolution)

   b) We are genetically programmed to take positive events for granted and pay them little heed – the primary function of the conscious mind is to keep us safe, so it focuses on identifying threats and things we need to solve.

And let's be honest, that 97% thing is REALLY common.

There's a plethora of good research data on this.

Several years after starting work on researching resonant leadership, Boyatzis and McKee (2005) returned to re-interview individuals who'd been best at it a decade earlier. They found the vast majority of them had reverted to dissonant leadership style.

They put the reversion down to leadership stress, the special pressure leaders feel because of the demands of power and of being in the limelight – there's no place for leaders to hide. Their financial performance is there for everyone to see, and their head is likely to be the first to roll if it disappoints. Moreover, the approachability that characterises resonance means they are constantly much more visible to everyone they lead than say an autocrat. (Boyatzis R and McKee A, 2005, *Resonant Leadership*, Harvard Business School Press).

Fortunately, we can learn hugely from how the minority of leaders who sustained resonant leadership for more than a decade did it. And that has zero, zip and nada to do with willpower. It turns out they all had some way of counteracting the negative programming impact of leadership stress on their behaviour. They all regularly included activities in their routine that provided positive psychological conditioning to nullify the deleterious impact of leadership stress. Readers may recognise this as a cognitive behavioural approach.

We see the same phenomenon in our surveys of former delegates. There's a concrete statistical relationship between how much our alumni put into actively managing their psychology, and the scale of improvement they report in their professional performance (and in their personal lives).

Eating pressure for breakfast needs to become an unconscious routine rather than a macho expression of bravado and hope. That comes from achieving deep psychological resilience, which in turn requires active management of the psychological environment.

Positive psychology research in recent years has proved that resilience is built when we spend time in positive emotional states. Whilst experiencing positive emotion we are constantly triggering the chemical and synaptic changes in our brain that manifest as increased ability to push through challenges, cruise past setbacks without losing momentum, and survive stressful and even traumatic experiences much more readily and completely.

Indeed resilience has been shown to determine whether we experience post traumatic growth or stress disorder following traumatic experiences. That is the reason the US Army has since 2009 trained all its NCOs as positive psychology coaches, under the auspices of Professor Martin Seligman, University of Pennsylvania, known as the father of positive psychology. Since when substance abuse, depression, post-traumatic stress disorder, and panic symptoms amongst troops have all been halved.

Leadership resilience is built in exactly the same way as general resilience. The way to achieve it is to stop trying to hold dissonant behaviour at bay with our force of will – that is always certain to eventually fail. The answer is to actively manage our conditioning inputs so as to optimise the amount of time we spend in positive states, and thus create the resilience we seek.

Positives in, positives out.

The benefits extend beyond leadership behaviour into all aspects of personal effectiveness. High levels of stress wipe out clarity of thinking, creativity, emotional intelligence, analytical reasoning skills, motivation and energy – and it feels very unpleasant. The health dangers of prolonged stress are well documented and can be extreme. Highly resilient people avoid these performance and quality of life killers more often than others. Even in high pressure situations they spend more time in high performance states and so, as the data clearly shows, they outperform others. And enjoy life more.

Lastly, in psychological terms, it makes no sense to try and reverse dissonance and performance collapse in the moment once they have kicked in. Not because the thinking behind wanting to put things right isn't appropriate. But because, sadly, it's already too late: no amount of will power and strength of character can enable the brain to do that. The cortex or part of the brain where our higher functions reside – including intellect, EQ, creativity – is closed down by a combination of the limbic system and prefrontal cortex as a result of the emotional highjack we have experienced. In simple terms, the kit we need for higher functioning is temporarily, and comprehensively, put into standby mode.

Furthermore, the hormones generated by the emotional flooding stress creates can take eight hours to dissipate from the system, and for the whole of that time one's performance and behaviour are impacted negatively.

The only reliable answer is to focus on creating a positively conditioning psychological environment that will build resilience. That's the smart place to invest your effort. The evidence is clear: this is the only approach that works.

Conditioning is everything a human being experiences. Its internal sources are our thoughts, what we say, reliving past events through accessing our memories. Externally, the list is longer: family, friends, colleagues, strangers, in fact just other people. What we watch and listen to – movies, TV, radio, podcasts, computer games, media in general. Everything we read: internet, novels, business cases, newspapers… You get the idea, it's a vast 24/7 multifaceted stream of data. And we are unconsciously programmed by it in a myriad of ways. If you reflect for a moment on how much of that is positive and reinforces the world view we would like those we lead to hold it can be a chilling experience.

Positive conditioning promotes positivity, hope, optimism, resilience, self-esteem, physical and mental health, longevity, relationships, influencing skills, organisational financial performance and on and on – all replicated research results. Negative conditioning has exactly the opposite impact. Positives in, positives out – it's easy to make a start by becoming mindful of what we allow into our brains rather than being a passive consumer of whatever happens to pop into our head, or out of our mouths, or be going on around us.

So we've come full circle. Positive conditioning creates resilient leaders who stay resonant when stuff hits the fan, and who exemplify your aspirational culture more fully more of the time. That resonance and enlightened values behaviour in turn preserves and promotes engagement. Engagement releases discretionary effort, and all of the value that creates flows straight to the bottomline. We don't have to choose people or profit, we only have to choose our conditioning, and that we can do.

## About Graham Keen

Graham Keen is an accountant and business psychologist. At his company New Impetus International he leads a team that creates long-lasting positive change in corporates.

He was a senior manager at *Ernst & Young*, a former plc CFO, and a corporate finance and M&A adviser.

More recently in 2003 he studied with Martin Seligman, the founder of positive psychology, and is a certified *Authentic Happiness Coach* and a Chartered Member of the *International Positive Psychology Association*.

This unique combination of skills and experience has given him deep insights into business leaders' issues and objectives, and how you can use applied psychology with confidence to implement pragmatic real-world solutions. His book *Positive Leaders, Positive Change* is to be published by *Rethink Press* in 2019.

With 24 years' experience advising more than 250 corporate clients on leadership, ethos and profitability, Graham now works with complex international organisations across EMEA and beyond delivering enlightened cultures and financial growth.

*www.grahamkeen.com*

*LinkedIn: https://www.linkedin.com/in/grahamkeennewimpetus ?originalSubdomain=uk*

*Facebook: https://www.facebook.com/NewImpetus*

*Twitter: https://twitter.com/GKeenNewImpetus*

# Leaders And The Five Acts Of Love

## Steven Shove MBA, DipM

*"Where there is love there is life."*

Mahatma Ghandi

## Why a chapter on love for leaders?

The answer is twofold:

Firstly, because love is the foundation and engine of every sustainable successful venture and secondly, because the role of leaders has the greatest impact on the world. Leaders and how they love has an impact on performance, our personal wellbeing, society and nature, with consequences that extend far beyond the immediacy of our own environments and into the future too.

Love is good and goodness should be the pursuit of every leader! An ideal but nonetheless one I believe in.

When the subject of leadership is viewed through this particular lens, leaders learn that they have a tremendous responsibility a) to love, and b) to facilitate and nurture love in others.

I wrote a chapter in *Fit For Purpose Leadership #4* entitled *The Really Wild Leader* which included love as one of the most notable characteristics of an exceptional leader. It included Richard Branson's view on the matter alongside my own thinking as to why it is such an important quality. In the chapter below, I expand on this topic.

In business terms, it is true that leaders and their enterprises can succeed without love; perhaps by sheer determination or because of fleeting market opportunities for instance, and even by luck. But it is a fact that success will not last without love; and it will be more limited in its impact.

Why? Because love is a creative and powerful force that offers continual and renewed energy. It is the stuff that keeps us going! Without it, atrophy will ensue, and all ventures will ultimately perish. Consider the fate of any relationship, society or project that has not been driven by love and the passion to succeed.

This is borne out by Newton's second law of thermodynamics which states that, "... *without a suitable energy source, over time and within a closed system, entropy or disorder will increase as usable energy is converted to unusable energy".*

Loving leadership therefore, should be considered as the energy source, like the sun; strong and brightly shining. The very energy needed for success. The stronger and longer a leader's love can burn the more things will flourish.

So, love of what exactly? How to love and how to direct it?

To answer these questions, I have identified five acts of love, to serve as a guide and support to leaders and others in any position of influence.

These are not romantic definitions of love but definitions that I believe will provide the basis for successful leadership in the 21st century; which sees the world facing incredible competition, worsening physical and mental health, changing political systems, the skewed transfer of wealth and power, impending climatic disaster, the emergence of technologies that could be used for tremendous good or bad, and the breakdown of too many facets of society. The responsibility on leaders is immense!

A conscious and deliberate consideration and focus on the right acts of love by those that have the greatest impact on our world (our leaders!), can make all the difference.

Love has never been taught at business school. It has never been part of an MBA programme. Perhaps now, it is time that it should.

## The Five Acts of Love

I have classified love for leaders into the following *Five Acts of Love*. Each is important in its own right but, like the acts of a play that build throughout a production and lead towards a climax in the final scene, each one builds upon the other before it.

- Self-love
- Love of others
- Love of the natural environment
- Love of what we do
- Love of how we do it

If we excel in achieving love further up the scale (1-5) but fail to do so in any of the preceding categories, our performance and the impact of our actions will not be optimal or as long lasting. This will also be the case if there is a random mix of love across a number but not all of the categories.

If, however, we secure the foundation of each one in order so that they are all achieved, then our results can be fantastic, and lives made truly amazing. I call this, *The promise.*

So, let's break each of the five acts down a little to explore a number of their attributes and how each act of love can be realised.

The first act is the act of loving oneself.

## Act 1. Self-love

This may be defined as regard for one's own wellbeing or happiness or being kind to oneself. It is in no way to be defined by such words as conceit or vanity, for these will destroy good rather than create it.

If you want your results (the fruits of your labour) to grow and be sustained, I argue that self-love is a pre-requisite.

And, if you do not actively love yourself you will be far more likely to neglect your own security, physical and mental wellbeing and personal development. This will be to the detriment of all other things, even those things that you hold most dear.

Through neglect you will not be at your best. This can result in far less being achieved than might be possible. It can result in errors and poor decisions being made, opportunities or threats being missed, and can ultimately even lead to your early departure from the position of influence you cherish.

As leaders we have been given the most golden opportunity to influence others and the world around us. It would be a shame to waste it through lack of self-love!

So, I recommend, be good to yourself:

- Eat well and healthily
- Get sufficient rest and quality sleep
- Exercise
- Be authentic and true to yourself to shape your work or change your environment to align to your values
- Nurture your talents and skills

- Surround yourself with wonderful people
- Take care of your mental and emotional health
- Take time for yourself and to be with loved ones
- Seek help or support when needed from those you trust and who care for you, and
- Spend regular time in nature

We all instinctively know what we must do but quite often fall short of knowing how to do it, especially with busy schedules, interruptions and demands. There is no simple answer other than it takes discipline, and to be disciplined, that takes motivation.

People are either motivated mainly by fear or by reward. Leaders will know where on this spectrum they fall.

If leaders imagine the best or worst-case scenario of what they might or might not otherwise achieve, given the current regard or love they show for themselves, then this might encourage them to take the actions necessary to fulfil their potential. They may perhaps even reframe what it is they might be capable of achieving, if only they more actively choose to give themselves the attention they deserve.

Ask, how could I more actively love myself to improve my personal levels of wellbeing and happiness and to hone my capabilities? To whom or where might I go to for advice and support? Who will hold me accountable? If I looked after or invested in myself better than I do today, who or what might benefit from my actions, by how much more and for how much longer?

And now onto Act Two – *The Love of others.*

## Act 2. Love of others

Ultimately, a leader who does not love people will not get the best from them. We will not serve them to the best of our abilities and we will not grow.

To love means to have a deep feeling of affection or fondness.

So, how do leaders demonstrate love to the people around them and how do teams respond when they feel loved or cared for? And isn't this all a little bit *airy fairy* in the cold and hard world of commerce and other performance driven environments?

To love people is not *airy fairy!*

If you want great results achieved with more consistency by a motivated, innovative and dedicated team, they need to be loved.

Research backs this up in studies that show what happens to people when they feel loved compared to when they do not:

- Their mental health becomes stronger
- People's physical health improves
- People's behaviour becomes more constructive
- Their performance improves and becomes more consistent

So, what can leaders do to show greater love for their people – teams, suppliers, partners and customers alike? The answers are common to all relationships.

- Being attentive to the needs, wellbeing, behaviours and feelings
- Encouraging people to develop, to try new things and to persevere
- Adopting a positive attitude, tone and engagement
- Being honest and operating at all times from a position of integrity

- Avoiding the creation of any unnecessary sense of insecurity
- Being firm but fair and consistent in your behaviours and leadership
- Respecting, valuing and supporting each person as a unique individual
- Actively listening and showing that people are being listened to
- Demonstrating flexibility when you can if this will help someone cope or thrive
- Be kind – there is no room for bullying!

Ask, how do I demonstrate love for the people with whom I work or serve. What is the impact of my doing so? What about those you never meet whose lives are affected by your choices? Whose society are you impacting and how?

Asking people how they feel is the most powerful tool of all. When did you last do that?

Once love is established for yourself and for others, then the capacity to extend our love further beyond the immediacy of ourselves can be tremendous as it affects the world more widely. Now that we have love for those nearest and dearest to us, we can share our love more widely.


## Act 3. Love of the natural environment

In the past and within indigenous tribes today, every leader will have demonstrated a profound love and appreciation of the natural world. They will have understood not to take too much. They will have recognised the need for sustainability, and they will have used any resources with reverence, respect and care. They will also have accepted short-term hardships or change in order to protect longer term needs.

So, why is this not the case today?

The answer is quite straight forward. People in the modern world have simply lost touch with nature. They have become too far removed from it and the consequences have become dire. Furthermore, decisions are made with immediate short terms results in mind, with a very local mindset as to the impact of any decision and perhaps a sense that one's personal impact on the world may not be that great anyway.

In my role in developing leaders I have the privilege of travelling to far flung places around the world to teach survival skills and apply the lessons learned back to their personal, business and academic lives.

On a recent deserted island off the coast of Borneo I gathered several kilos of plastic waste off one beach in just half an hour. The plastic was useful to me in terms of survival skills training but terrible to the local wildlife.

On the mainland of Borneo in Sabah I had the good fortune to travel the Kinabatangan river. Looking forward to seeing orangutan, crocodiles, wild birds, elephants and all manner of other exotic wildlife, I found that the primary rain forest was just thirty metres wide on either side of the river. Beyond that were thousands of square kilometres of barren palm oil plantations. Furthermore, tribal people all-over South East Asia have lost their abundant and healthy jungle-based livelihoods and had them replaced by modern day lives of poverty or dependence on overseas plantation owners. It is a very sad sight to see.

It is now time for modern leaders to resume the mantle of environmental protector. Love of self and others is arguably quite futile if we do not ultimately also actively love the natural world and the societies of all living beings too, wherever they may be in the world.

The responsibility for leaders to protect the environment therefore represents an incredible duty of care. It is one that unhappily, is still too often limited to published statements of corporate social responsibility which too often serve as little more than a PR exercise or regulatory tick list.

So, what should modern leaders do?

Leaders have the following responsibilities to:

- Learn about the environmental consequences of their decisions or choices – at home, further afield, now and into the future
- Educate their staff, suppliers, partners and customers about the impact their choices and their combined supply chain have on the environment
- Act to change policies, procedures and practices to ensure the best environmental decisions are being made

Leaders always need to question what they are doing, why they are doing it and how they are doing it. When asking these questions though, they must now always consider the environmental and social consequences in arriving at their answers.

The challenge can seem quite overwhelming with short term performance goals never receding, and with so very much to change. Do not be disheartened!

With every leader beginning to factor in love of the environment into all their decisions, the benefits will collectively be huge.

Leaders all have a sphere of direct control and a wider sphere of broader influence. Start with what you feel comfortable with. Begin by working with like-minded people and teams who will innovate, adapt and progress the environmental journey with you, and perhaps even use your mission to attract the very best people to your teams and companies. The green movement is becoming mainstream and as with any and all situational changes, exciting opportunities arise too!

What can you do today to bring a more active stance to loving the environment into your work today?

A wonderful resource to getting started is provided by the B Corporation, an organisation that helps businesses meet the highest standards of verified social and environmental performance. *https://bcorporation.uk* A great place to start!

We have looked at ourselves, others and the environment, so let's now look at whether we actually love what we do.

## Act 4. Love of what we do

I began this chapter by referring to the power of love and its ability to provide the great energy needed to continually lead with success, but how many people do you know that truly love what they do? And how many of those are leaders?

If someone really loves what they do, they have endless energy and optimism. Their determination is driven by joy and a positive belief that what they are doing is right. It is right for them, for their people and for the wider world or environment and society as a whole. They are unstoppable! Is that you?

If not, then no matter how hard we work or how diligent we are in our duties, regardless of how deeply we care for ourselves, our people or our world, we will likely suffer from a number of challenges that may ultimately undermine our ability to perform at our best with any consistency we will likely suffer, over time, from a number of challenges.

Our energies will be diverted and become less potent.

When I speak with leaders who do not love what they do, they frequently suffer from one or more of the following:

1. Low energy
2. A lack of fulfilment
3. Difficulty in concentrating and an inability to focus
4. Feelings of conflict
5. Anxiety or depression

6. Unhappiness

7. Short term thinking

8. Physical illness

So, what can a leader do if he or she recognises that they are not in love with what they do?

The answer is simple in the telling but perhaps a little more difficult in the making as it requires brutal honesty and a recognition that not all is well.

The answer is to change what you do.

The modern working world is now full of professionals who have decided to change what they do, and plentiful with those that have embraced a new role or career. Fortune favours the brave!

Ask, do I love what I do? All of it? Some of it? Consider how you feel and to what degree you ascribe to the eight symptoms listed above.

There may be small changes you can make, or it may be a bold move that is needed.

A common desire I hear from leaders and their teams is to have a greater purpose to their roles and to have a wider impact on the world. A wonderful way to achieve this is to lead your organisation into becoming a business for good. *B1G1* is a superb organisation that allows your company to support the united nations global objectives. I highly recommend it. Take a look at *https://www.b1g1.com/businessforgood*

Insofar as is possible, I urge my clients to follow what they love, to set out making the right choices at the outset and at every key juncture of the career, or changing more bravely many years later, when they realise that the path they have chosen is not now the right one.

I also advise that leaders ensure they have the right people in the right jobs, not just because of technical skills but because of passion and their respective love of the role too. Loving what we do can be tremendously fulfilling but loving how we do it too can make it overwhelmingly so.

## Act 5. Love of how we do it

Loving how we do things is almost, if not equal to loving what we do. If we feel conflict in how we do things through our behaviours or choices, this leads to a lack of love and the very same negative symptoms as above.

What and how! Both represent a missed opportunity for wonderful people to be great.

I have met several amazing leaders who have been at odds with how they have been required to run their businesses or operations, whether they have found themselves beholden to new investors or driven by a variety of other reasons. Where pressures are placed upon them to act in a manner contrary to what they feel is right they will not love how they are made to work. Again, through lack of love, their energy will be lessened and their capability to achieve over the long term will be curtailed.

If you are a leader suffering in this regard, you need to address the root causes or be prepared to change your circumstance. It is something I have personally experienced. I changed my circumstance despite my fears and benefitted from the change incredibly.

If you are leading others who feel this way you may need to reflect on whether it's you or they that needs to change or become more accepting. The results will be worth it!

Ask, what conflicts do I have regarding how I am required to lead or run my operation? What are the consequences for me personally, for others, for society and the environment? Are there any things I need to change about how I expect others to work for me and why?

## Conclusion

Remember the indigenous leaders who truly understood their impact on the environment and the superior performance of those who love themselves, what they do and how they do it and who have a genuine love for other people too. They are like the energy of the sun and able to achieve great things. They are also a force for good.

In conclusion, love is powerful! It provides the energy and understanding necessary for the long-term success and well-being of people, our organisations and of the natural world.

To be fit for purpose, the five acts of love cannot therefore be overlooked. Each one requires conscious thought and action by every leader, which on occasion may require a little bravery too.

## References

- Sherry Rauh (January 2009)10 surprising health benefits of love
  www.webmd.com/sex-relationships/features/health-benefits

- Jamie Ducharme (February 2018) Ways Love is Good for Your Health – Time
  http://amp.timeinc.net/time/5136409/health-benefits-love

- Mellisa Vallas MD (March 2015) The positive effects of love on mental health – Psychiatry Advisor
  www.psychiatryadvisor.com

- Harry Levinson (July 1996) When Executives Burn Out - Harvard Business Review
  https://hbr.org/1996/07/when-executives-burn-out

- George B. (2008). Discover your True North. John Wiley & Sons.

## About Steven Shove

Steven is an experienced business leader and performance coach, a respected thought leader and one of the UK's most highly qualified survival instructors who passionately applies the principles of *"original human success"* to businesses, teams and individuals seeking to thrive in today's ever demanding and increasingly competitive environments.
For nearly 30 years, Steven consulted to and successfully led a variety of international teams and businesses, improving performance across the myriad of business functions and industries but specialising in leadership, sales, business strategy and personal development.

Steven is CEO and Founding Director of the *Really Wild Group* that offers performance improvement coaching and consulting services, educational events, executive retreats, camps and expeditions to the business, education and leisure sectors.

Steven and his teams deploy a powerful and proven methodology for success called the *Really Wild Method®* that uniquely equips and enables individuals and organisations to thrive and deliver superior performance with far greater consistency and predictability - in the most exciting, engaging and memorable of ways.

Today, Steven works with clients in the boardroom or classroom to remote places such as the Arctic and the jungles of the Amazon and Borneo.

*www.reallywildeducation.com www.reallywildbusiness.com*

*LinkedIN: www.linkedin.com/in/stevenshove*

*Facebook: Steven Shove and Really Wild Education*

# Every Type Of Business Must Become Its Own Media Business

### Mike Hax Hacker

A quick look at any successful business reveals an interesting trend. They are producing more and more content to digitally market their business.

This content growth has led to the *Attention Economy*. Consumers are literally being bombarded with content which has led to an evolution in response. We are becoming immune to any content that appears in our social media feeds, emails and internet particularly if not relevant to us.

Our attention and ability or desire to consume content now goes through a conscious filtering process at the point immediately we see it.

Take a moment to observe how quickly you scroll through a *Facebook* or *LinkedIn* feed. Study how quickly you swipe through these posts and also observe what makes you stop and study a title, description line, a photo, or even video that makes us pause on that post.

Ask yourself, *why did I stop on this post?* You'll find, that in someway the post is *relevant* to you. Maybe not specifically to your business but it may tweak your curiosity as a point of news, something that resonates in your home life, your family or indeed something you know or feel might be of interest to you or someone else.

Current technology and the subsequent developing innovations has allowed us or indeed encourages us to change our digital consumption habits. I would argue that a good percentage of this is in the subconscious. Speaking from my point of view I have certainly noticed that I spend more time scrolling through to my main social media and news feed platforms more times in a day then I ever found myself reading magazines or newspapers. Including how I filter television. Whether we like it or not we are being swept along this cascading digital river, much like a twig travelling down fast flowing stream. We have content being delivered at our fingertips and are adapting our lives and habits so that we consume the digital content if it's relevant to us.

There is no doubt that any successful business has learnt to understand this and is leaning towards its influence. Hard selling is a thing of the past. You can see how television advertising has adapted and how big corporations are now leveraging their stories and their client stories to interact with potential clients. There is evidence that these business-es are now adapting to the way in which consumers research information and shop for product.

Building audiences is the key.

The buyer is now in complete control. Advertising and sell-ing techniques that were working as little as five years ago have now been pushed back into the annals of history. Those old methods are simply non-productive. This consumer trend has driven a desire for relationships albeit that they are either passive or active relationships. By that I mean passive to be following and observing, and active to be more engaging and responsive.

Because the buyer is in control now more so than ever it's important that business controls what can be read or researched about them online. It is critical therefore to deploy ones own content. The more we put out there that comes from us the greater the chance a prospect will consume content that is positive and not something negative from someone else.

The only way any business, despite its size can build and maintain a viable market presence in the digital world is to approach this *content* marketing strategically. This principle may not be new, but the approach has changed so fundamentally that *Old School* ways just don't hack it anymore.

We have to lean into the changing digital trends.

I believe that there is now, more that ever, a wider dividing line between marketing and sales. The market place is now demanding that business approaches the consumer to build a relationship step by step. Anything less and we switch off because its too sales orientated.

Media agencies understand the need for customer relationship in order to generate qualified leads for their clients. Their strategic approach to creating content is driven by building relationships. Traditionally, businesses that allocate adequate marketing budgets are the ones that can afford media agencies to work for them. But what of all the businesses who don't employ media agencies nor provide adequate budgets in marketing for business growth? How do they or should they cope?

In my experience, I have found that there are three main reasons why any business does not attribute enough resources to their marketing. The first is missing the fundamental business basic of the importance of marketing and its relation to lead generation. The second is the structure of the business simply does not tribute time to plan and think strategically. And the third is that any marketing conducted is usually poorly planned and poorly executed.

The outcome is disappointing non-productive results.

It's hard to find a business in today's digital landscape that doesn't have an online presence and therefore producing content is unavoidable. From simple emails through to newsletters to social media articles, sales funnel and websites, All require what is now commonly understood to be *Content*.

If a business cannot afford to employ a media agency to support them in their marketing then the business itself needs to look internally to produce the content. If it can't afford the financial commitment to employ someone to do it then it needs to devote time as its investment. The owner or an employee of that business will have to produce that required content.

Words, photographs or video - *especially video* - are the key content instruments.

Having or learning the skills to produce content that is most productive is also a significant part of the required investment. *Business Basics 101* teaches us that marketing produces qualified leads and those leads convert to buyers through the sales process. Ergo any content produced and deployed into the public domain sits firmly under the *marketing* umbrella. Again, our new attention economy is demanding that all content we produce must be superior to our competitors otherwise we simply lose the lead through lack of engagement. Let's face it, engagement leads to trust, trust leads to loyalty and loyalty leads to sales.

Maintaining a viable digital presence that nurtures an audience builds trust and encourages loyalty also requires regularity and consistency. This of course necessitates forward planning to sustain the production of all this content.

Of course, the written word is easier than say photographs and photographs are easier than video. However, there is plenty of evidence pointing to video, the more complex content to produce, is also the most productive. Initially, words may be the more financially viable tool, however approaching content production in a media management way will allow for growth and therefore an escalation into photography and video. That said, fundamentally any business has to choose the right content that is the most productive to its audience.

Every business from a plumber to a car mechanic to a large size trucking company must look at producing content to feed their digital presence and nurture their audience. The production of that contents needs to be adequately planned so that it is strategic, relevant, and above all engaging to the people its intended for. It's the only way it will be productive.

Richard Branson, I believe once observed that successful businesses will spend approximately 10% of their turnover on marketing but a business in deliberate growth will spend anything up to 25% of its turnover. Of course, some business models will spend far more, by the very nature of their business, but generally this has proved to be the case.

You have to devote enough time and resource to maintain a regular supply of digital content. Of course, this will differ largely depending on the business, nevertheless in the *attention economy* the production of such content in some measure is necessary and even unavoidable. This means that all businesses have to approach producing this content as a fundamental part of their business operation. This means that the content produced not only has to be relevant and engaging but it needs to be fresh and frequent.

I believe that more so than ever now despite what any business does by way of service or product, in order to market successfully they have to first become a media business. Why? Because as I have said already, producing productive content has to be approached strategically. It needs to align with the brand, with its market audience and be ahead of its competition.

This means it plays an unavoidable part in the all important aspect of lead generation. Above all for it to work effectively in any sized business it needs to be sustainable.

To approach the production of content to fit all of the above criteria, the creation of that content has done properly and systematically. I believe the only way to do this is to approach it in the same way any media business would, for itself or its own clients.

This is done:

*Strategically,* by identifying overall objectives, identifying and maintaining brand values and producing content that is fit for purpose.

*Objectively,* by considering a campaign approach for specific initiatives, albeit public relation or sales. This should be done through adequate planning that is time sensitive, with clear short-term and long-term objectives.

*Productively,* by ensuring that there is a sustainable production pipeline in place that is supported by the best people within the organisation. This even works for a sole entrepreneur by learning how to produce the content and by ensuring there is enough time to produce and deploy that content themselves.

Any professional media business would approach all of the above by identifying potential content, allocating adequate time and resource to create that content and then have known methods of deployment that fit the content's specific objective. Objectives could be reinforcing expertise, sharing something of value, even sharing the benefits of a specific service or product. And then, by ensuring the consumer is taken on a simple and friction free journey to the call to action and beyond.

Approaching production content for entrepreneurs, small businesses or enterprise must happen in the same professional manner in order to compete in this attention economy. In my view, it is more important than ever that for all business to be successful it must become a media business first.

Leading *that* change is critical.

## About Hax

Hax is an experienced filmmaker, he help organisations find the stories that engage their audiences and stakeholders.

His name is Mike Hacker, but he's known as *Hax*. His work has been seen on the *History Channel, Animal Planet,* and *AETN Group,* including the *Crime and Investigation Network.*

Hax has many years' experience working with corporates to create videos that deliver real benefits for business. He now works across every area of video communication – internal communications, compliance, on-boarding staff, marketing, communicating change.

Video content has a critical place in any communications strategy and is invaluable for organisations wishing to build relationships and communicate better.

Hax believes the nature of communication and marketing has changed. People spend more time online and communication is becoming much more visual. Everyone can research any of us online, looking for our values and our credibility *before* they contact us. We need to pay attention to how we come across in that initial research.

Stories are the key.

"As a film and documentary maker, with my experience I delve into my subjects to uncover their stories. By understanding the goals and objectives of your business, you can formulate a strategy to maximise your return on investment."

Hax can be contacted through *Prisma Broadcast,* at:

*hax@prismabroadcast.com*

# The Real Business Of Charity: Where The Head Is Just As Important As The Heart

## Sophia Giblin

I never imagined that one day I would be the Founder of a thriving children's charity. I believe that often our life assignments choose us, rather than us choosing them.

When I was 15, my Mum tragically passed away from cancer. It was a very short battle with the disease. By the time they caught it, it was too late.

She left behind my Dad, myself and my three younger siblings. I was in the middle of my GCSEs, at that time of life where we're asked to make big decisions about the route our lives will take. All of my friends were getting excited about the subjects they would take at A-Level, which would lead them on to follow their passions at degree level, ultimately propelling them into the career of their dreams. While my friends were moving on with hopes of what was to come, I felt there was no future for me. I just wanted to go back in time to when my Mum was still here.

My Dad told me that I should go to University and study business so I could get one of those *nice little marketing jobs* that apparently existed. I went to the closest University to my home because I was petrified of being away from what I knew.

I couldn't identify it at the time, but I was crippled with anxiety following my Mum's death. The world had gone from being a place of great opportunity and excitement to a place where heartache and loss were at the centre of my experience.

Despite the crushing fear I pushed on by putting one foot in front of the other and got my degree in Business Administration.

I tried to find the *nice little marketing job* I had been promised, but as I graduated the recession hit. Graduate jobs were few and far between and there was no way that I was an outstanding candidate for any role.

My heart wasn't in it.

I started looking to the other people in my life for some inspiration. My cousin had started to train as a Play Therapist when we were in our early twenties. I'd never heard of Play Therapy before. She told me that it was like counselling for children where they use toys and games instead of talking. She explained that children often find it hard to talk about events that have been traumatic and instead they just need to *play it out*. This helps them to find some way of expressing the way they feel without using language. Instead they could use art materials, puppets, sand, music, clay or dressing up to show how they are feeling in a way that feels safer than talking.

It instantly clicked. Play Therapy was the support that we needed as children following the loss of our Mum. This would have been especially appropriate for my youngest sibling who was only 9 at the time.

As a 15-year-old I was expected to deal with the loss as an adult would, only I didn't have the words to express how I was feeling. All I knew was that I felt sick all the time. Now I know that was the anxiety that I was living with daily, but I couldn't explain that to someone with words. If I'd have had some creative outlet with a trained person who was able to understand my feelings, I would have been able to grieve my loss as a teenager rather than remaining stuck in my trauma.

A fire lit up inside me. I hadn't realised that there was anything that could have been done to help children like me and my siblings, but as soon as I saw an opportunity to help others in similar situations, I knew that was what I had to do.

With this new found enthusiasm and passion I took the brave steps to set up my own charitable organisation at the age of 23. I was just a young girl with a fire in her heart at the time, with a degree in business but no real experience. I made it my mission to show up every day and put my all into building the charity, fuelled by the desire to help other children. I set up *Clear Sky Children's Charity* to provide Play and Creative Arts Therapy to primary school aged children who had experienced difficult early life experiences such as bereavement, abuse, bullying, fostering or family breakdown.

I went to train as a Play Therapist so I could deeply understand the needs of the children I wanted to serve. Through the process of training as a Therapist I started to heal the wounds of my own inner child and process the deep feelings of grief that I had been carrying around for years.

There's no manual for running a charity. The majority of what I do I have learned on the job. My passion for the work has always shone through above and beyond anything else, so I've never been scared to ask for the help that the charity needs. I've also become good at recognising when I need help myself and getting out of my own way to make sure that the needs of the charity always come first. I have been so lucky to have learned from some amazing people along the way. One of my favourite things about working in the charity sector is that most people are sympathetic to your cause and want to help in whatever way they can.

Turning tragedy into something meaningful has healed me in so many ways. I believe that we can all turn trauma into something positive if we believe that we can make a difference. I set out on this journey because I knew that I had to do something to help other who were hurting. I made the service to others my main focus and in turn I healed my own inner wounds in the process.

To know that the work of *Clear Sky* has made such a difference to over 500 children, some of which have required intensive one-to-one therapy, is something that makes me so proud and also humbles me. I feel genuinely honoured to have been able to create something that has touched the lives of these children, and I feel privileged to have been part of the healing journeys of many.

In retrospect, my Business degree has served me incredibly well in setting up and running a thriving charity in times of austerity where there are huge amounts of competition for funding. Clear Sky goes from strength to strength each year. I believe this is down to a few key factors that are pertinent to running any business.

## Understanding the needs of the people you are serving

It has never been more apparent that we are facing a mental health crisis. Increased media coverage of the importance of mental health has supported our mission and this trend is not slowing down. Sadly, the trends in poor mental health in children are not slowing down either. There will always be a need for specialist support services in this area.

Society seems to be slowly accepting that behavioural approaches to trauma can compound the issue. We now understand that the *stiff upper lip* does not serves us when it comes to mental health and that we need to tackle these challenges head on.

### Having an adaptable but solid business model to match market conditions

We are always adapting the delivery of our services to meet the changing needs of the children and families we serve, and the political landscape that we deliver our services in. We are always looking for new ways to meet the needs of our beneficiaries. This was initially all done through one-to-one therapeutic work, then in the form of training professionals, then through the introduction of parent groups.

Now our services also include online training for parents and a membership body for professionals so we can increase our reach and impact thousands of lives on an international scale through our own unique insights from a creative therapy perspective.

### Diversifying revenue streams and spreading financial risk

I think there is often a misconception about how charities operate. People often ask me, *"So, do you do everything for free then?"* The answer is *no*. We can't. Free doesn't enable us to scale our support and help more children and families.

As a charity we fill a very important gap in state provision.

The sad reality is that the waiting list for children to access specialist mental health services through the NHS are up to six-months in some areas of the UK. So yes, we do make a charge for our services so that we can continue to deliver our much-needed support in a sustainable way.

We do, however, subsidise a percentage of the work we do through fundraising so that it is more affordable for the schools we work with. This way, schools and funders have assurance that our model is robust enough to be sustainable. Without this, a charity risks become a black hole for funding and ultimately the desire for funders to keep financing the project dies down over time. This is where I have seen many other charitable organisations struggle to keep up as the Founders spend all of their time chasing money through fundraising to keep the project alive rather than focusing on the delivery of services in a sustainable manner.

Charities have to run on sound business principles. The business of charity required us to keep our head and our hearts aligned so that we can see the big picture at all times. If we spend too much time working from the heart on the delivery of the work, the financial or operational aspects may suffer. If we spend too much time working from the head on the business of the charity, the quality of the services we deliver may suffer. We need to maintain an equal balance of passion and pragmatism at all times. One doesn't work without the other in charity.

If you have a cause you believe in, make it your business to serve others by providing something you would have wanted in a time of need. You can do this through volunteering, through taking up a Trustee role in a charity you believe in or by setting up your own project.

If you're interested in starting a project, first think about how you could differentiate support in your local area to meet a need that's currently being overlooked.

Focus on quality of outcomes over quantity and make sure that you measure this diligently to prove that you're making a difference. Finally, focus on service of others by leading from the heart and you won't go far wrong.

## About Sophia Giblin

Sophia Giblin is an award-winning Charity Founder, Play Therapist and Entrepreneur who is passionate about children receiving emotional support for trauma as early as possible to prevent mental health difficulties in later life.

Sophia's focus is on educating parents in how to become agents of change for their own children through play and connection.

Her online *Treasure Time* courses walk parents through simple play activities for a stronger connection between parent and child which is the foundation for good mental health.

*www.clear-sky.org.uk*

*www.treasuretime.co.uk*

*https://www.linkedin.com/in/sophiagiblin/*

*@sophia_giblin (Twitter, Instagram)*

# Vulnerability And Your Leadership

## William Grover

I was born into an ordinary working-class family. We grew up in the sleepy seaside town of Hythe in Kent. My Dad was a salesman who worked long hours mainly in the motor trade and my Mum was a stay-at-home work-around-the-kids hairdresser. A *mumpreneur* in modern speak. She taught me so much about hard work, juggling multiple balls in the air whilst keeping everyone happy.

One of my earliest memories was of me sitting on the kitchen draining board at preschool age, watching my Mum make small talk with her clients, set perms, do blow-dry after blow-dry, trim after trim, all whilst keeping me entertained, our four cats and umpteen guinea pigs in order, the washing situation under control and getting the dinner ready for when my brother would return from school and my Dad would triumphantly come home after a day hustling at the showroom.

The smell of perming lotion and peroxide still evoke such strong and fond memories for me of those times when as a child I sat and thought to myself, *"How does she do it all? It looks like such hard work!"*

Sharing that time with Mum taught me so much about having a strong work ethic and it also opened my eyes to the concept of sacrifice and struggle for others. My Mum was the one I saw struggling. In between all the craziness of her weekdays she would steal a brief moment of her own for a quick cigarette and a *cuppa*, so as to steal herself for the next client or chore in her relentless diary. She swallowed her own personal feelings and problems to make sure her clients and family felt welcome, looked after and secure. She kept her own vulnerability tidily packed away like an inconvenience. It taught me to keep my feelings away from the outside world. For their sake and for my own.

To compound this learning, I would see my bright and brilliant Dad bowl in the front door every evening, cheerily greet us all without a care in the world and ask Mum, *"How was your day?"*, and she would dutifully reply, *"Lovely, how was yours?"* And then I would notice the glint in my Mum's eye that seemed to say, *"If you only knew the half of it."*

I had seen her work and sweat her way through the day, and even at that age I recognised her struggle. I saw how she had disguised it in her duty to serve others.

I think, in my early years, I must have decided three things:

- Never let them (or it) grind you down
- Never let them know when you struggle
- Choose a life in sales as it looks easier than being an entrepreneur or stay-at-home parent

Let me address each of those points now:

Point 1 on the list was impossible to accomplish. No matter how hard I worked or how many different work environments I found myself in, there were always set-backs, failures and moments when I just wanted to throw in the towel. Often, I would actually throw it in, and seek a different job with seemingly better-suited challenges to my skillset, or lack of skills. I was being ground down by life, work and my personal failings.

Point 2 I was damned good at. Instead of letting my colleagues or boss know when I was struggling, I became adept at hiding poor sales results behind high activity levels, and a cheery exterior. However, the cracks would start to show, and I would need to move on before they found me out as the failure I knew I was.

Point 3 turned out to be just wrong. For me, a career in sales wasn't easy at all. Even when I was experiencing success in relative terms, I would beat myself up if I wasn't top dog in every month. In a competitive industry, and one in which back then there was a high level of bravado, bullying and banter, there was no room for slacking, failure or feelings. I was definitely struggling and the effects on my physical and mental health were troubling. I was tired, confused, frustrated, disappointed, isolated and lost. I wasn't broken, but I was badly fractured. I knew something had to change.

My *way out* of that caustic existence happened gradually thanks to a long and often difficult combination of self-discovery, coaching, personal development, retraining and lots of sharing and understanding my own vulnerability. By tirelessly connecting to my fears and frustrations I was able to tune-in to the real me, figure out what was important in my life and learn to feel at ease with myself. I saw fear-based drive replaced with passion fed activity. I noticed the *just give it a shot* attitude start to bear fruit in every aspect of my life. Plus, by sharing my vulnerability with others, I noticed that they would do the same in return, and their levels of bravery and honesty would increase as feelings of loneliness and fear would subside.

Later, as a Coach, I began to see many clients in executive and leadership roles coming to me with a few similar issues:

- Feelings of isolation
- Failure to get strong buy-in from their teams

- Low levels of trust within their teams
- High levels of imposter syndrome

When working with one particular mastermind group of nine business owners who had some or all of the above challenges, I wondered how my own discoveries could help to form a solution for them and their teams. They helped me put together the structure for an experiment in mastering vulnerability. They got to work on it just one week later.

It wasn't long before the group were seeing interesting and exciting results. The group were encouraged to follow a process based on their own vulnerability, and use their findings to enhance their understanding of themselves and then in turn, create stronger teams within a more robust work culture. Here are the steps that they took.

## Acknowledge your vulnerability

They discovered that as a leader, first you must acknowledge you are, or have felt vulnerable. Your own vulnerability may come in the shape of a fear of failure, of making bad judgments, in feelings of isolation or thinking that all the responsibility is on your shoulders. Feeling that you need to have all the answers when you know you don't have them. That what if people find out that you have been blagging your way through life and that some one will eventually find you out. What if a competitor proves to be stronger and more innovative than you and your business and it all falls apart? Comparing yourself to others or having crazy expectations of yourself.

Acknowledging your own vulnerability is the first step to mastering it and using it in your favour.

## Give yourself permission to be vulnerable

Next, you must give yourself absolute permission to have those feelings of vulnerability that were covered earlier.

It is not simply enough to know that it has been a thing you have suffered in the past. More, that it is a thing that will and does happen in your life and work and it will continue to feature in one form or another. When you expect something, it takes away its power to blindside you, or at the very least shortens the impact of the surprise element it can carry.

## Thank your vulnerability

Listing your mistakes and fears is one thing that many of us are all too good at. Learning from them though, is a key to success. The clients were asked to list any and all the themes of their own vulnerability they could remember over their }careers, and then to uncover the positive intention each one of those challenges had for them. It is my belief that every negative emotion or action has a positive intention. This part can be extremely tricky if, like me, you adopt a naturally positive and forward-thinking attitude to life. However, the group came back with insightful discoveries such as, *"I realised my imposter syndrome was driving me to gain new qualifications and to work hard to help my teams succeed"* and *"when I look back now, I can see that feeling isolated did make me truly value the close friendships I have"* or *"my fear to take risks protected staff jobs".*

One member of the group even realised that there had been a direct link between his workaholic years, his subsequent ill health and then his embarking on a healthier lifestyle. It started the process of them seeing what these perceived weaknesses, setbacks and vulnerabilities had taught them. It was definitely time for the next step.

## Share your vulnerability

For some, this was an easy step, the only challenge for those few was going to be sharing vulnerability purposefully and not just as part of a general chitchat over a coffee. For others, the thought of sharing their vulnerability with anyone filled them with terror.

We began by sharing their stories of vulnerability within the group, and then gradually, pushing those out to their inner-circle of friends, family and colleagues. Whoever they felt they could or should share with. Many told the group of huge breakthroughs that had happened because of this exercise. People around them hadn't realised the problems they had been going through, and had wished to know sooner so they could have offered support or at the very least given some consolation. Colleagues thanked them for their lessons. Just by sharing their stories, they had engaged people on an emotional level and made the link between their own vulnerability and the basic human need for connection. Some magic was happening. Many of the group shared that they felt lighter and stronger through exposing their vulnerability.

The opposite of what they feared might happen.

## Promote vulnerability within your workplace

Following their own discoveries and benefits gained from the program, the group were then encouraged to share the process with their teams and colleagues. Yes, they encountered some scepticism before and during this roll-out, but because they had experienced the process themselves, and trusted in it, and with the help of each other, they pushed on. Over the weeks and months that followed they fed back some incredible gains:

- As leaders, they felt closer to their colleagues and part of a shared mission.

- Teams demonstrated higher levels of engagement at work and began forming closer relationships with each other.
- Meetings became more productive and solutions seemed to be easier to come by during challenging times.
- There was much less need for awkward HR confrontations as people were more open and honest with each other from the start.
- People were smiling more.
- Teams were arranging more socials outside of work.
- Productivity went up.
- Sales and profit increased.

Embracing vulnerability and creating a culture which promotes and encourages it had allowed an emotional connection to take place. That connection had given rise to trust, and from that trust came teamwork, engagement and commitment.

If I had worked in an environment like that from the start maybe I wouldn't have retrained and pursued self-employment. Maybe I wouldn't have spent years soul searching and working on my personal and professional development.

But you know what they say? Everything happens for a reason.

## About William Grover

William is a widely sought after and highly energetic Coach. His mission in life is to help people feel empowered, communicate more clearly and work better together. He is known for his tough yet playful approach to coaching and behavioural change work. As an elite Breakthrough Coach, NLP Trainer and Culture Change Consultant William feels at home working with whole organisations and its key individuals on a 1-2-1 basis. He uses innovative methods to define and cultivate meaningful change for his clients. William challenges the thinking and decision-making processes of his clients to bring about lasting changes and deliver powerful outcomes.

*www.workingonwhy.com*

*www.linkedin.com/in/workingonwhy*

*www.facebook.com/workingonwhy*

*Instagram: @will_grover_coach*

*Twitter: @willgrovercoach*

## It's Business, So... Make it Personal
### A funny thing happened on the way to freedom

### Barbara Khattri

I had a Problem, in fact more than one!

You probably know that feeling, the challenges of running a business, you're juggling everything, constantly under pressure, and trying not to drop balls?

Like many business owners the motivations for going into business for ourselves are fuelled by one of the following;

- a passion for our craft or product
- a desire to no longer be *micromanaged*
- the desire to create a workplace with a real *feel-good factor* where there is a culture of appreciation and the feeling (please excuse the use of the *f* word ☺) that YOU are needed for the value you bring

or

- the *illusion* or delusion that it will be easier to make money
- add into that mix the belief that we'll have more freedom, more time to do what we want and before you know it, you've got a fledgling Boss ready to take that courageous leap into what, despite all the ups and downs, is the best club ever!

Now for any of the above to have any chance of a positive outcome for the business, we should first have gotten some serious training in management, sales, marketing, HR and of course mind reading. ☺

If we're lucky we may have touched on one or two of those, but rarely the only important one, mind reading!

Typically, we start out as 'IT', the face of the business. We're the main 'earner' or income generator. Usually though we're also the bookkeeper, the marketer and product development innovator to name just a few of the hats we try to wear every day.

Soon we realise that we need more people, we've been having conversations like, *"I can't manage, there's only one of me,"* sound familiar? We then take that really big step of hiring our first person, and that is often in hindsight, the exact moment when things start to get complicated.

Of course it's human nature that we want to work with people that we like and so rarely are our first hires the people that we need, rather they are people who share similar passions or heaven forbid someone who can just work when we need them to, but rarely are they someone who would challenge us and enable the business to grow and thrive.

Now though we're **'IN IT'** and often that ends up being that we're up to our neck **'IN IT'**!

We're doing all that we've always done and now we're managing, or at least trying to, other people, who, it turns out are just as complicated as us. Even worse they're not mind readers either and before we know it, we start to feel out of control and then horror of horrors we try to control people. We start micro managing and setting up systems so that everything is done exactly *our way* and now instead of *"it's only me, how can I get it all done,"* it's *"well no one does it as well as me,"* or even *"I'd be better off just doing it all myself, no one else can do it the way I do anyway!"*

From this point it's only a short while till we realise that the *feel-good factor* is slipping, or we overhear one of our people speaking, well complaining about us, in the same way as we did our old boss. Genuinely we have no idea how with the awesome intentions we had when we set out, we'd end up here, as just another business that if we're lucky is surviving but is not standing out and thriving in the way that we so clearly had in our view when we started. That clear vision we had can surprisingly very quickly start to fade around the edges.

And there you have it, **Problem #1 - We've only taken our view of the situation.**

We said we wanted people, a team who would take responsibility, use their initiative and get the results without us checking on them all the time, but was that really what we wanted, or did we just want people who would do things our way, without asking and not think for themselves. That line *"I'm not paying them to think I'm just paying them to get the job done"* may even have passed our lips, followed by *"but I don't get why they're not passionate about what we do and how can they even think of asking for a holiday then, they know that's our busiest time!"*

Is any of this ringing any bells? ☺

By now if anyone even mentioned the word *culture*, we'd likely say, *"For goodness sake, don't talk to me about all that fluffy nonsense, I'm in business to make money, I need more customers, more cash, definitely more time and just for the record do you know how hard that is?"*

I guess if it was easy everyone could and would do it.

So, let's rewind back to where in my journey as the boss I had my light bulb moment.

I thought to myself, *Wow would I even want to work for me?* I'd wanted a business that has the feel-good factor every day,

I wanted freedom from my boss and now some of my team wanted freedom from me.

Freedom and responsibility, I realised are of course flip sides of the same card, you just can't have one without the other, and so if I want freedom and I want my team to take responsibility, they have to have freedom too.

But where does freedom or autonomy stop and anarchy begin, could it really work that we all get what we want insofar as how we do what we do and the business still get what it needs?

I took a step back, not by choice but by the fact that there was, as was often the case in those early years, a crisis! I needed a solution and a way to make my business better. I thought, if I strip it all back and look at it from every angle, what's the real nature of how I'm doing business?

And that was it, **Problem #2**, I wasn't, actually I couldn't **look at situations from every angle** on a daily basis, this was sounding a lot like **Problem #1.**

I was trying to fast-track my business to one that could thrive when it wasn't even set up to survive.

It's like I'd chosen to be alone on a dessert island trying to do all of the four key elements of survival alone:

- making the fire and keep it going
- finding the wood and making the shelter
- hunting and cooking the food and
- sourcing the fresh water.

Of course, there would be no time or energy to even think about a way to get off the island.

Trouble was that the dessert island scenario was of my choosing. Who knows if it was through fear or ego but what

I do know is that as soon as I changed my view, my world and business changed too!

**So, was it easy? No, but was it simple? Hell yes ...**

- it's simply connecting the **nature** of how we each do stuff
- to the **nature** of the stuff we have to do
- with the right **process** or **tool**
- and that means the right **stuff** gets done.

It's simply instead of having culture and business sitting on opposite sides of the fence, creating a culture camp where everyone gets what their superpower is, what makes them tick, and then where they may click or clash and then of course knowing how to choose to click better together.

So those four elements of survival are basically superpowers. It's not difficult to spot your superpowers; they are clearly distinctive, it's like wearing different caps that highlight the different roles. We're either:

- **The MOVER** inspiring and assertive, super focused on the details that make the difference and spotting what others miss,
- **The CONDUCTOR** competitive, organised and confident, used to getting projects over the line. Timing is everything,
- **The TRANSFORMER** motivating and creative, always spotting the next opportunity with many projects on the go. Great in marketing and product development, or
- **The SHAPER** supportive, patient, and most likely to be the person people come to with their issues. Great for HR or a culture role.

Funny thing with superpowers though, they can have us super clear on our own strengths, yet unable to spot the superpower in others. We often instead notice what we perceive as their weaknesses which are in fact their strengths.

Why is that? Well human nature can feel threatened by what's different. At work though when we stick with what's familiar and feels safe, we stay stuck in our comfort zones and before long there is no growth, in our own skills or the business.

Whilst we appreciate the end results of each other's strengths, truth be told, we can find those differences irritating, but taking that view will always hold the business back.

At work, even as the boss, we just make up part of the team.

How we can best complement and support each other is largely based on how well we see ourselves. If we need to be right, rather than get the right result, that's the example we'll set for our team, therefore the business results will be as fragmented as the behaviour of us and our team.

So, what's the solution?

### A Better Business 'Connected Model' a

# Culture Camp

Where the Nature of Your Business works in Harmony with the Nature of YOU and your TEAM

| The TRANSFORMER | The CONDUCTOR | The MOVER | The SHAPER |
|---|---|---|---|
| VISION MOTIVATION & CREATIVITY | COMPETITIVE ORGANISED & CONFIDENT | FOCUSED ASSERTIVE & COMMUNICATIVE | INTUITIVE SUPPORTIVE & PATIENT |

So, **Problem #3, 'how we see, measure and leverage the value in others points of view'** again a lot like **Problem #1.**

It's that simple, its simply *Changing Your View* and trust me it's a lot easier than constantly struggling to survive.

The ripple effect is that we no longer lurch between one of these three things;

- The communication thing. Where balls are getting dropped with those little misunderstandings, where you know you want to listen, but they just take so much of your time to resolve.
- The responsibility thing. Where sales and booking opportunities are being lost because my team aren't or don't know how to take the initiative, or
- The customer experience thing. Where who cares about the balls, you're losing money and customers, or clients simply aren't coming back.

Instead I'm now 'ON IT'.

I'm able to work on the business, to build the assets and grow the profits.

Now it's:

- **Training,** delivered in the right way to the right person who gets the right results.
- **Autonomy,** our team delivering on our values and getting the right results.
- **Customer Experience,** solutions that ensure customer and team loyalty that are getting the right results.

So, what was holding me back from building a *Connected Culture* in my business? Was it:

- **The TIME** thing, making the investment in what I didn't know?
- **The BELIEF** thing, it all sounded great, but would it work for me? Or was it
- **The VALUE** thing, in the past measuring the ROI of culture on profit had proved elusive.

It was probably a bit of all three I'd say!

So, what's the impact now, on me, the business and the team on a daily basis?

Well there are always new challenges and pressures, the speed of change can be overwhelming and dropping balls today can mean a business won't survive tomorrow. Our culture though has removed that fear, that sense of isolation, and the real cost, our sleep, our time, our money, our freedom. The difference that makes the difference is trust, I now influence and empower the team to give their best, so the business now gets their best. We meet in the middle, we're in it together.

So, where's the best place to start? Well, from where you are now! The sooner you start the sooner you'll have a thriving business that's not dependent on you, a business that's a go-to, experiential destination, a legacy business that brings you the freedom to one day be **'Out of It'.** ☺

The biggest challenges in the change process, the transformation, can be facing where our nature, our superpower, can be as much a hindrance as it is an asset. Letting go of any *ego stuff* and really trusting the superpowers in our team solves all three problems. We get that vital 360° view and the opportunity to get off that dessert island once and for all! However, this can bring out a resistance around our beliefs about what being a Boss means. What's on the other side, is the freedom that **self-leadership** brings. It transforms staff into a high performing team, it's truly inclusive, brings back the feel-good factor and fast tracks connecting our **People** and **Purpose to our Profit.**

We use phrases with our teams like *you've gotta get in the game* etc, but if it's a game, surely, we've got to make it more fun. A **Connected Culture** at the heart of the business makes it so and gives that vital positive edge.

After all, it's business so **Make it Personal** and bring the dream of why you started your business back into reality, cos your freedom depends on it!

## About Barbara Khattri

Barbara is a *Connection Coach*. She builds cultures from the bottom up, which enables everyone to be the difference that makes the difference. Her belief in the power of communication, conversations and community are what connect purpose, people and profits. This however is underpinned by the strength that each individual's  relationships and family connections gain by being part of the *elaworld* community.

Barbara is the founder of *elaworld*. *The Business Culture Awards, Consultancy* for 2019 and owner of elements *Lifestyle Salon*, an award-winning business and culture academy. She is also a *National Apprenticeship Ambassador* and a passionate lifelong learner.

*elaworld* is based on principles learnt through working with Tibetan rug weavers in Kathmandu and 35 years business experience.

Barbara's driving force is being the mother of three sons who are now digital influencers and is supporting other families to redefine and build a new style of family connections.

*www.elaworld.world*

*https://www.linkedin.com/in/barbarakhattri/*

*https://twitter.com/barbarakhattri*

# Leading The Collaborative Sale

**Kim Newman**

The world of business has changed and continues to change dramatically and rapidly and the need to be agile and collaborative has never been more business critical. All business leaders and owners are now in the business of sales because being known, liked and trusted continues to grow in importance and relationships now form the firm foundation for profile, pipeline and growth in most service based businesses.

Back in the early days of my career working in large consultancies, customers were a necessary evil and got an *off the shelf* service, your focus was achieving productivity targets and fee recovery rates, we didn't have time to speak to clients to understand their problems or challenges and co-create a bespoke solution, all creativity and enthusiasm was completely stifled.

As soon as I set up my own business, 24 years ago now, that was the first thing that I changed. I didn't want PML to be perceived as just another consultant that isn't interested in them, tells you the time on your own watch and adds little value.

Our environment dictates how we perform and this now necessitates the need for new attitudes, new leadership skills, and a new understanding of how to approach customers. This step change will have been very obvious in a lot of industries, competition will have changed and out of the box solutions will have become much more difficult to differentiate and sell let alone demonstrate the added value that will be provided.

The upshot of these market changes is that our services have a shelf life and very quickly become commoditized. As leaders, we need to constantly develop and evolve how we provide services and fully understand the changing needs of our clients. Agility and differentiation are the only way to be successful in today's market place. This is a challenge that collaborative selling allows you to fulfil.

## Traditional Approach to Sales

The traditional approach to selling by telling customers what you can offer them and making their problems fit your services is long gone, likewise the focus on volume based *pile it high and sell it cheap* approaches.

Traditionally, little time or attention was paid to targeting markets or planning sales conversations with a customer. It was all about the *numbers game,* a generic pitch was made to as many prospects as possible as quickly as possible and that enabled you to tick a performance box.

The sales process focused on a persuasive pitch, manipulative closing techniques, and the salesperson's skills in handling customer objections. High performing salespeople were those who had mastered the art of arm-twisting. Hard to believe that this often resulted in a resounding *no thank you* response!

The traditional sales pitch had to be generic. All of the features and benefits had to be covered because there was no way of knowing what was important or even relevant to the customer. It was a true scatter gun approach of trying to sell everything to everyone in the hope that something would hit the target and a sale would be made. There was no follow-up or learning process to seek to improve understanding and future performance after the sale, just move on to the next pitch.

Traditional selling is not dead. It is still used in a few industries. Despite market changes, some organisations are still insulting their customers with high-pressured, traditional tactics. They are short-term thinkers who assume there is an endless supply of new customers despite the reputational damage that a traditional sales approach may bring.

Is this the basis for robust long-term relationships? Is this a formula for business success? Absolutely not. It does not take a genius to realize that the focus in traditional selling is misplaced and shortsighted.

It does not encourage referrals, references, repeat business, word-of-mouth advertising, customer satisfaction or good will.

## Collaborative Selling

Collaborative selling has an entirely different mindset fueled by agile leadership, clear purpose, strategy and objectives with a clear commitment to the long-term and creation of a win-win outcome.

Today's customers buy differently, customers are more interested in great relationships. Today's customers are looking for measurable quality and value in the services they buy. Today's customers are looking for long-term relationships with leaders and organisations who they know, like and trust and who invest the time to get to know them. Collaborating companies are also maximizing the benefit of this approach in terms of efficiencies in working practice and streamlining of processes.

Strategic alliancing, partnering, collaboration call it what you will is taking place throughout the world on a macro level (industry to industry) and on a micro (business to customer) level.

Collaborative selling means handling every aspect of the sales process with a high degree of leadership professionalism and planning. There are six basic steps that describe how the collaborative sales process unfolds:

- **Target** - The first step is an absolute necessity: understand exactly what problems the customer has within your target market and what they need to address it then adjust or design your service accordingly. It takes some time, but careful planning focuses effort and efficiency and provides a greater return on time and money invested. Collaborative salespeople know they must concentrate on prospects who have a high probability of buying. Think of it as replacing the scatter gun approach with a laser focused approach that is more effective with a single targeted shot as opposed to multiple random shots.

- **Contact** - The first step after customer targeting is to contact them in a cost-effective and professional way. Get to know and understand the individual, their interests, hobbies and drivers to build rapport. This will be a combination of online and offline approaches but the right combination of contacting strategies will ensure that a high perceived value is created before meeting with prospects. When contact is made, a collaborative approach will set the stage for a cooperative, working relationship. Issues and challenges should be clearly explored to fully understand what is important them. A desire to explore needs and opportunities should be clearly articulated which will build credibility and trust and competitive advantages can then be shared without jumping into a presentation. Resist the urge to leap in with solutions and proposals until the clients priorities are fully understood.

- **Explore** - Once issues and challenges have been explored and the customers priorities have been clearly understood you can start to explore methods and solutions to address the customers needs. The key focus must be on addressing the customers needs or challenges not what services you can sell.

During the explore stage, collaborative leaders and organisations conduct research, meet with their prospects frequently, and do whatever it takes to become an expert on their prospect's business. This information and intelligence is best captured within a Customer Plan which then provides an ongoing point of reference and focus. The give-and-take relationship that develops sets the stage for in-depth exploration of options that may culminate in a sale.

Collaborative leaders and organisations make it clear that they want to help, not just make a sale. If, after information-gathering, collaborative organisations find that their services are not appropriate for their prospects, which should be unlikely due to, careful targeted marketing, they will forego the sale, but will have made a long term friend and business contact that they can stay in touch with and meet again in the future.

- **Collaborate** - It is at this point after an in-depth exploration of a prospect's situation that collaborative organisations talk specifically about their services in the context of prospects' needs or opportunities. Collaborative leaders never dictate solutions to their prospects. Instead, they form *partnerships* in which prospects play an active role in the co-design of the best solution in the spirit of *let's work together on the solution and together build a commitment to its successful implementation.*
  This team-approach to problem-solving ensures that prospects will be committed to solutions. By making customers equal partners in problem-solving, collaborative selling addresses objections and reduces or eliminates the risk that is inherent in the customer's decision-making process.

- **Confirm** - Bear in mind that, in every phase of the collaborative selling process, proactive and positive communication should have taken place to ensure clarity of understanding. Collaborative organisations will then move on to the next phase of the sales process only after they have received assurances that their customers are in agreement with them on everything that has been discussed and communicated.

This agree-as-you-go process eliminates the need to *"close"* the sale or handle objections. Most objections will have surfaced long before this point and been addressed. If resistance does occur, the organisation simply gathers more information or clarifies a detail. With collaborative selling, the sale is essentially a matter of when and not if. Confirming the sale is the logical conclusion to an on-going communication and problem-solving process. There is no need to *close* them. Customers will commit when all their buying criteria are met!

- **Assure** - This phase of the collaborative sales process begins immediately after the sale has been confirmed. Collaborative leaders will keep in contact after the sale.
  They communicate regularly about dates and timetables and other relevant matters. They make sure their customers are satisfied. They help customers track their results and analyze the effectiveness of the solution.

Collaborative selling is the key to differentiation - it represents a focus on quality and customer satisfaction. It reflects a high degree of professionalism and a primary focus on relationships rather than transactions. It is clear that collaborative selling is a win-win situation, one that provides increased security to both parties. This increased security is exactly what customers want and need given the rapidly changing world we find ourselves in.

Implementing collaborative selling across the business or the organisation is the leadership challenge.

## About Kim Newman

Kim has over 25 years experience having originally qualified as a surveyor and then progressed into a variety of roles with national management consultancy practices. Since 1996 she has been the founder and co-owner of PML, a leading consultancy and advisory business that works with organisations and leaders to give them the skills to collaborate more effectively with their staff, teams and customers to create and maintain win:win business relationships.

Kim Newman is an established business leader, business improvement and collaboration specialist to the public and private sector and was proud to be awarded an entry in the *Who's Who of Britain's Business Elite* in 2009. She is also the Chair of *Orwell Housing Association*.

Kim is an experienced adviser, trainer and mentor and is passionate about giving something back and constantly looks for ways to improve and develop her business by working collaboratively with others.

*Linkedin - linkedin.com/in/kimnewman7*

*Twitter - KNewmanPML*

*www.pmlgroup.com*

*Collabor-8 Scorecard - https://collabor-8.pmlgroup.com/*

# Whose Business Structure Is It Anyway?

## Stuart Ritchie

It may seem trite to ask the question which business structure you should use as anybody with a business will have already made that decision.

But has that decision been made casually or is it one made with complete advice? Has thought been given to the extremes a business owner may face – namely realising significant value on a sale of the business or the depths of despair when business solvency is in issue or extensive litigation is in contemplation or underway. Put differently, has a decision been made in default of considering all the options available?

And to what extent has consideration been given to business structures which allow others to invest in your business or those which allow you to motivate key members of your management team?

As is well known, the classic business structures are:

- Sole Trader
- Partnership
- Limited Liability Partnership ("an LLP")
- Limited Liability Company ("a company")

The pros and cons of each business structure will be familiar to most entrepreneurs and are set out below. The key difference is between trading personally, either as a sole trader or in partnership, or through a corporate entity, such as a company or an LLP.

| Type | Structure | Pros | Cons |
|---|---|---|---|
| Sole Trader | Exclusive owner of the business, entitled to keep all profits but liable for all debts | • Low cost, easy to set-up<br>• Full control retained<br>• Very little financial reporting | • Full liability for debt<br>• Pay more in tax<br>• Lacks credibility in market |
| Partnership | Between two or more individuals who share management and profits, but are individual partners liable for all partnership debts | • The above, but with more hands<br>• More potential to raise finance | • The above, affecting all partners<br>• Can be messy to wind up |
| Limited Liability Company | Private company whose owners are legally responsible for its debts only to the extent of the amount of capital they invested | • Less personal financial exposure<br>• Favourable tax regime<br>• Can work for corporate clients | • Administrative and regulatory demands heavier<br>• Annual accounts and financial reports must be placed in public domain |
| Limited Liability Partnership | Some or all partners have limited liabilities, and exhibits elements of partnerships and corporations | • Flexibility: can be incorporated in members' agreement<br>• Advantages of limited company and partnership combined | • Profit taxed as income<br>• Partners must disclose income<br>• LLP must start to trade within a year of registration – or be struck off |

**Table 1 Advantages and Disadvantages of Each Business Structure**

With companies and LLPs comes, as the names suggest, protection from financial liability due to the separate legal personality of each type of entity. This downside protection is significant in that if the entity becomes insolvent, any liabilities in excess of assets are owed by the insolvent entity rather than by you as either the shareholder/director of the company or as a member of the LLP.

Enough of the downside – now for the upside of different business structures.

### The Holding Company (of a Group of Companies)

Holding companies of groups of companies are popular with entrepreneurs with multiple business interests and where liability protection is sensible. They are also typical where larger business groupings exist. A classic structure chart for a group of companies is set out below. This may apply within a single jurisdiction, such as operating exclusively within the United Kingdom, or will sometimes work across international borders where separate subsidiary companies are established in each country where there are operations.

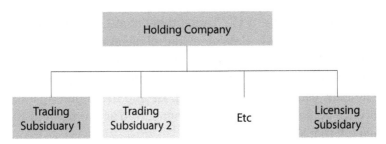

**Table 2 The Holding Company (of a Group of Companies)**

There are a number of advantages:

### a) Recognising distinct businesses

Many entrepreneurs do not set out to create a group of businesses but over time as the ideas flow, there can be several businesses whose product or service lines are very different from each other and the objectives for each business differ significantly. In such circumstances, these businesses are best held in separate companies and the entrepreneur may choose to hold all their business interests in a single group of companies or multiple groups of companies.

### b) Ease of disposal

A service line or product line can more easily be sold if held in a subsidiary company, as it is the shares in the subsidiary company which are being sold. The alternative is a sale of assets and separating out those assets being sold from those being retained can be a more complex exercise.

### c) Patent Licensing

Intellectual Property ("IP") and other patents may be held by industry or territory. Retaining control of your IP is incredibly important and as your business expands, you may consider keeping all your IP in your holding company or a subsidiary company established for that purpose and then entering into licence agreements with your other subsidiary companies to exploit that IP.

### d) Tax Advantage

Selling the shareholding in a subsidiary company should be exempt from corporation tax in the UK (under present rules known as the Substantial Shareholdings Exemption). For a serial entrepreneur this gives a great advantage in that capital can be built up within your holding company with successive sales of subsidiary companies.

Profits within a group of companies can be paid to the holding company tax free as tax will have already have been paid by the subsidiary company on its profits. And if your subsidiary company is loss making, those losses can for tax purposes be set against the profits made by either the holding company or other subsidiary companies.

### e) Risk Management

When businesses are properly categorised and administered within a subsidiary company, financial claims such as for trading losses, product or service line liability claims are against the subsidiary company only. This may be especially important if riskier operations are being considered as they can be separated from the core business.

For larger businesses, holding companies of groups of companies can be a compelling proposition.

### Alphabet shares – flexibility in sharing out profits

Whilst partnerships and LLPs have great flexibility in how profits are distributed, the same cannot be said of companies. Other than the payment of remuneration, which can be directed to those who work in the business, rewards to shareholders normally follow the owners of the shareholdings in the company.

This is because when most companies are formed, they create just one class of shares, usually called ordinary shares which means if a dividend is paid, every shareholder gets the same payment for each share they own.

However, you can create different classes of shares, usually called alphabet shares, in which case shareholders get paid a dividend according to the class of share they hold. A classic structure chart for a company with alphabet shares is set out below.

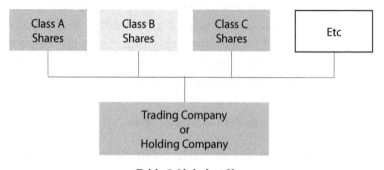

**Table 3 Alphabet Shares**

Dividends on alphabet shares can, subject to any other considerations, be directed to the shareholder with the lowest marginal rate of tax. Dividends on alphabet shares can also be directed to the class of shareholders where the shareholders' agreement decides who should receive a dividend in preference to any other class of shareholder. This is a common occurrence when shareholding classes represent the stage of investment by a shareholder or the division between the involvement of the shareholder as either management or an investor, which is often common in private equity type scenarios.

## External investors

Most entrepreneurs will have watched *Dragons' Den* or *The Apprentice* with some degree of fascination as to the process of bringing in third party investors to their business.

Sometimes the investor brings much needed expertise and sometimes provides the finance a new and growing business needs to capitalise on its business opportunity.

Most countries recognise and therefore incentivise external investment into entrepreneurial businesses. In the UK, this is achieved through a number of tax reliefs available to external investors using:

- EIS - the Enterprise Investment Scheme
- SEIS - the Seed Enterprise Investment Scheme
- VCTs - Venture Capital Trusts

EIS and SEIS allow investors to inject money into individual companies selected by the investor with tax relief being given on the amount invested – SEIS getting more tax relief than EIS but on smaller amounts invested. VCTs are investment trusts that invest in a range of small trading companies selected by the VCT's investment manager with tax relief being available on the amount invested and also when money is realised.

A classic structure chart for a company with *external investors* is set out below – the investment may be into ordinary share capital or alphabet shares.

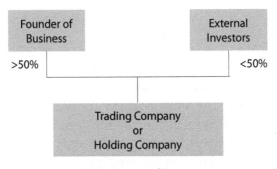

**Table 4 External Investors**

## Exit planning for the business owner

The long term significance of selecting the right business structure for you is that if your ambition is to sell the business, how can you do so with the least amount of *Capital Gains Tax* being payable?

Most countries incentivise entrepreneurs with a reduced tax rate when they come to sell their business. In the UK, this is achieved by reducing the *Capital Gains Tax* rate to 10% when *Entrepreneurs' Relief* applies.

*Entrepreneurs' Relief* can apply to the disposal of a business held personally as a sole trader, as a partner in a partnership or an LLP or on the sale of shares in a company. The detailed conditions for *Entrepreneurs' Relief* are complex and early and continual advice is essential to avoid losing the benefit of the reduced tax rate. However, if properly planned, a tax rate of 10% on up to £10 million of capital gains realised by an individual taxpayer in their lifetime can be achieved.

*Entrepreneurs' Relief* will therefore be the key concern for business owners contemplating a sale of part or all of their business. Not only will getting the right price on a sale be important – so will making sure the 10% rate for *Capital Gains Tax* applies to the gain on selling the business.

## Author's Note

The decision on which business structure is ultimately yours and is often nuanced by the importance placed on the competing factors of simplicity and complexity. The size of the business will have a bearing on the decision as well as the extent of the business activity. And if asset protection is of importance, then building up wealth either personally or in your holding company will be paramount.

## About Stuart Ritchie

Stuart Ritchie is a chartered accountant and chartered tax adviser with over 30 years' experience. He is the tax partner with *Ritchie Phillips LLP* who provide specialist tax advice and accountancy services in four areas: private clients and private wealth, entrepreneurs and growing businesses, resident foreign domiciliaries and tax disputes and investigations.

His three decades of experience allow him to provide a unique insight into the circumstances of individuals and families and the objectives they seek to achieve to grow their wealth and their businesses and in time pass it onto their heirs and successors.

For more details:

*www.ritchiephillips.co.uk*

*www.linkedin.com/in/stuartritchiefca/*

Stuart is also the founding partner of *My Accountancy HQ* which provides data driven cloud accounting for small and growing businesses.

*www.myaccountancyhq.co.uk*

# Seven Ways To Retain Talent

## Linda Hill

At the age of 15, I took home economics as a subject at school. I was expecting to learn how to cook and bake the perfect scones. What I did not expect was to learn about Maslow's *Hierarchy of Needs and Self-Actualisation*.

Mrs Radloff made it her mission to teach her students much more than what the syllabus dictated. She was one of those exceptional teachers. You know the kind of person you remember years later, even though your paths never cross again. These individuals make an impact on us, inspire us to achieve and help us to be the best version of ourselves.

If you think back on your journey, how many teachers or leaders stand out for you? Someone who motivated and inspired you. My guess is only a handful. These people influenced us, pushed us out of our comfort zone and believed in us.

Because of this we excelled and produced our best work.

As leaders we have the opportunity to inspire others and help them achieve beyond what they might think they are capable of. Great leaders are able to spot talent and develop their teams or employees to achieve at their optimum level.

At times it can be challenging finding the right person for your organisation. Someone that fits the culture, has a strong work ethic and can adapt to change. How do you go about finding the right person with the required level of expertise when there are financial constraints and only a moderate package to offer? There are ways to attract the right people, even with a restrictive budget.

When advertising the role focus on why your company would be a great place to work. Job ads tend to be one sided and often it's all about the skills of the candidate. Highlight how future employees can benefit from being part of your team. Bear the *WIFM* acronym in mind - *What's in it for me?*

Put yourself in the shoes of the employee and what benefits could be of value to someone apart from their pay cheque. Perhaps ongoing learning opportunities to develop their skill set or flexible working hours to accommodate children, looking after parents or support other responsibilities?

We have clients who attract the best talent as they have created a culture where people want to work. Company perks include being able to trade in holiday days and take sabbaticals to fulfil bucket list dreams. Think what perks you could offer your employees and how you can use it as a tool to attract and retain staff.

Being able to make good decisions and choose the right team members when recruiting will have a great impact on the growth and success of the business. Getting it right can be challenging as we want the best possible outcome based on the information we have. Learn to trust your instincts. It can help you when you have to choose between two candidates and when difficult decisions have to be made.

When doing interviews, be yourself. We all have our own unique style. Some prefer a more formal and structured interview. I have found that when I put people at ease and make them feel welcome, I get to know them better during the interview. Try different ways and see what works best.

Ultimately the interview is about getting to know the

person and to establish if they will be a good fit for the business. Be mindful of how you feel straight after the interview. Did the candidate leave you feeling energised and positive? If not, they might not be the right fit for your organisation.

I always ask candidates why they want to leave their current role and based on their answers I share seven guidelines to retaining your staff.

## Valued

Make staff feel valued and that their efforts are appreciated. Empower them and let them take ownership. Ask their opinion and involve them in the decision making. On a daily basis your staff is in the front line dealing with your clients. They have an excellent sense of what your clients want or how things can be improved to provide an even better service.

When employees don't feel valued, they will look for work where they feel their talents are appreciated.

## Autonomy

Don't micromanage but let people do the roles you pay them for. The lack of freedom breeds frustration and leads to a lack of trust.

Steve Jobs sums it up when he says: *"It doesn't make sense to hire smart people and tell them what to do; we hire smart people so they can tell us what to do."*

## Transparency

Be transparent during the hiring process. If the role is misrepresented there will be unrealistic expectations and staff won't stay. Don't make promises during the interview process you cannot commit to. Provide clarity around the package on offer so the prospective staff member can make an informed decision before accepting the job. Share the mission and vision of the company to ensure goals and values are aligned. This will result in mutual respect and staff will stay longer.

## Gratitude

Remember to say thank you and acknowledge when someone has gone the extra mile. People want to feel you care even though you are paying them a salary.

Staff appreciation is an integral part of motivating and retaining staff. Saying thank you increases loyalty, improves productivity and creates a positive working environment that leads to longevity in the workplace.

Great employees will eventually leave if they feel they are being taken for granted. It was William James who said, *"The deepest craving of human nature is the need to be appreciated."*

## Development

Ensure that people don't stagnate in their roles but continue to grow and develop. Instill in your staff a mindset of continued learning. Nelson Mandela said, *"Education is the most powerful weapon which you can use to change the world."*

Constant improvement is key, and you want your staff to progress and evolve. This will contribute to the success of the business and fulfilment of its people.

## Support

A lack of support can lead to an employee feeling overwhelmed, under achieving and potentially resigning. Focus on people's strengths and provide support and encouragement. Assign a mentor to new starters. This will nurture them and help them thrive in their new position. The right mentor will provide accountability and help the new staff member to integrate seamlessly within the organisation. Don't under -estimate the effect the mentee will have on the mentor. The relationship will have an impact on both parties and the mentor will benefit through personal growth which in turn will have a positive impact on the business and longevity within the organisation.

## Fun

Think of all the jobs you've had since you started your working career. Which one did you enjoy the most? Chances are that the job you have fond memories of is the one where you worked with great people. Individuals stay longer in roles where there is teamwork, camaraderie and an element of fun. Create an environment that supports this as team spirit is an essential ingredient for performance and success.

As Andrew Carnegie said, *"There is little success where there is little laughter."*

## To conclude

We all have different leadership and communication styles but when looking to recruit, remember this:

Don't miss out on great people because of being too focussed on having every boxed ticked. Many of us know of someone who is highly skilled but currently unemployed. We know they have much to offer a company and would be a great asset but they don't tick every box. This means they miss out on interviews where they can prove their worth. Be that leader who can recognise when someone is smart, willing to do whatever it takes to succeed in their role and have the right attitude and mindset to serve your customers.

## About Linda Hill

Linda Hill is the founder of award-winning recruitment agency, *Linda Hill Recruitment*. Since 2004, she has been mentoring candidates on how to progress their careers and help companies attract and retain talent. As a qualified teacher, international speaker, business owner and author of *Beauty Therapist to Entrepreneur: the essential guide to accelerate your career*  *success*, Linda's career strategies develop people to achieve beyond what they think they are capable of.

*info@lindahillrecruitment.co.uk*

*www.lindahillrecruitment.co.uk*

*www.linkedin.com/in/lindahillrecruitment*

*Beauty Therapist to Entrepreneur* is available on Amazon

*https://www.amazon.co.uk/Beauty-Therapist-Entrepreneur-essential-accelerating*

# Dynamic Leadership In These Disruptive Days

## Claire Croft

Ask what it means to be a *good leader,* and most of us would be able to provide a halfway decent description. For many people, notions of leadership are rooted in traditional cultural archetypes. We might imagine a king on his throne, surveying his subjects and his land, ruling with the implacable iron fist that has been his family's stock in trade for centuries. Or the brave warrior, leading his troops, powered by a deep sense of conviction. Many of the leaders we venerate directly reflect such archetypes, regardless of context. In politics, for example, Churchill embodies the king, and Margaret Thatcher the warrior ("this lady is not for turning").

Against this backdrop, new theoretical modes and models of leadership have sprung up as frequently as most of us change our socks. But a core belief underpins most of them. It is that there is a *gold standard* for leadership, a sort of platonic ideal that we all need to be taught. *Henley Business School* alone offers eight different programmes on leadership - implying that the development journey is vast, life-long and uniform. Indeed, rather like consumer goods advertising, business schools and others have sought to convince insecure professionals that they do not already have it within them to perform at their best. This line of argument is helpful if you want to make money from learning and development. How well it serves the business community is another question altogether.

I am going to argue that a definition of leadership that is rooted in static, idealised archetypes is not fit for the world in which we now find ourselves.

Few would question that there is sufficient evidence to suggest that we are all working in more complex and challenging environments than ever. For example, in their 2013 paper *Technology at Work*[1], *Citi Group* estimated that it took 75 years for the telephone to reach 50 million users. By way of contrast, *Twitter* took just nine months, and *Pokémon* nine days.

Many of us in business live in fear of being overtaken by events, technology-related and otherwise. *The Katzenbach Centre* conducted a survey of more than 2,200 executives, managers, and employees around the world[2]. Almost half of the respondents reported that their companies didn't have the necessary capabilities to ensure that change is sustained in the long term. And that's just the change that people know is necessary - not future events that we can't predict.

What does this mean for leaders? In simple terms, the pace and nature of today's working world demands a more dynamic and adaptable form of leadership. The world is now too complex for any static, one-size-fits-all leadership mode or model to stand a realistic chance of success. And, even if it could, there is an additional problem: we are all individuals with different strengths, weaknesses and preferences. What works well for one might not for another.

Dynamic leadership can be defined as **the process of activating our own potential in accordance with the needs of the present moment.** The key to it is to be found within the individual. It is focused not on the pursuit of some unattainable standard of excellence. Rather, it is grounded in the value of the individual as a creative, adaptable, unique and resilient source of inspiration and guidance for others. Such leadership involves constant vigilance around our own behaviour, and nurturing of our best selves.

Dynamic leadership is also essential for the health and wellbeing of the leader. A life spent in pursuit of some abstract gold standard drains energy and self-esteem. But by embracing a more individualised sense of what leadership is, we can focus on bringing the best out of ourselves and helping others do the same each and every day. It's an enabler to sustaining performance, precisely because it delivers frequent, energy-giving moments of achievement.

Having said that, leading dynamically isn't easy. And it is often difficult to know where to begin.

As a start point, in my work with high performing leaders and teams, I invite leaders to reflect on their own adaptability and capabilities in the context of three principal performance factors. These factors are supported by decades of research into organisational performance. Mastery of them predicts effective leadership in almost any circumstances. Note that this isn't a model, more a collection of foundational concepts that can help the leader interrogate how effectively she is leading in a changing world.

The first is **contextual clarity.**

*Key question: Are my people 100% clear on why I'm making these requests of them?*

All good decisions start with clarity on context: it is shocking how absent this is from many workplace conversations. People are also forgetful, easily distracted, and prone to making up their own narratives. We are all meaning-making machines (and more so than ever given the complexity of the world of work). In the absence of frequent and effective communication, we will often make up the wrong meaning.

So, the dynamic leader will ask herself: am I making it my mission to communicate the 'why' time and again, so that everyone understands the essence of the journey we're on? And, when circumstances change, how quickly and effectively am I communicating this?

The second is **agenda alignment.**

*Key question: To what extent do my people feel connected to the vision of the business each and every day?*

It is clear to most of us that vision is important. But this is not just a question of having written one - *PowerPoint* charts and words on walls change nothing. The dynamic leader will identify the extent to which people buy in to that vision in the course of their daily work, and are able to connect their work to it. All of us tend to see our lives in pixels, and lose the big picture. What's more, in complex organisations, the relationship between the macro and the micro might not be clear. Dynamic leadership seeks to correct this by making constant and meaningful connections between the work of today and the world of tomorrow.

A related consideration in this context is conflict management. It is important to emphasise that having aligned agendas doesn't mean everyone is going to agree all of the time. All businesses are a composite of different points of view and priorities. The dynamic leader understands that managing tensions in ways that lead to better outcomes is a prerequisite of progress. She knows that conflict is healthy. She does not foster conflict for the sake of it (or for political or entertainment purposes). But she permissions it where it serves the work, and seeks to strike a healthy balance between debate and decisiveness.

The final factor is **creative capabilities.**

*Key question: Am I empowering all my people to solve problems, think critically and generate ideas?*

The dynamic leader empowers everyone through the organisation to imagine, make and deliver the changes that growth depends on. A critical ingredient to this is irreverence. So, she will ask herself: can my people question and challenge what they perceive to be wrong or in need of improvement, or am I allowing sacred cows to hinder progress?

Another element is *risk tolerance*. Although it is an almost constant presence today, organisations tend to find it challenging to embrace ambiguity - for the simple reason that the unknown represents a potential survival threat. To compensate they will either consciously or subconsciously cling to ways of thinking and acting that are known or that have worked in the past. Unfortunately, this avoidance behaviour and can, and often does, negate the potential for success. To thrive, the dynamic leader leans into problem solving. But trying to solve problems without tolerating risk is little more than tinkering around the edges. So the dynamic leader will ask herself whether she is good at embracing failure when new things stutter and fail, or instead defaults to embracing blame.

Together contextual clarity, agenda alignment and creative capabilities are the foundations of dynamic, resilient, adaptable leadership. Why? For the simple reason that they focus not on a single behavioural mode or model, but on identifying and addressing the fluctuating forces that influence team performance, in real time, as they occur.

The transition to dynamic leadership can be emotionally challenging, and often feels lonely. But it needn't be so. To manage it, leaders need to focus within, pursuing self-knowledge and building on strengths whilst also addressing weaknesses and blind-spots. At the same time they need to remain connected to the needs of their firm and their people.

They need to prioritise nurturing and developing the quality of their engagement and conversations with their organisation above all else.

Dynamic leadership is now table-stakes for developing and managing any complex organisation. Without it, you can all but guarantee system-wide failures of strategy, expectation management, people alignment and communication. With it, you stand a chance of being able to avoid them, and enjoy a richer, more rewarding working life.

[1]https://www.oxfordmartin.ox.ac.uk/downloads/reports/ Citi_GPS_Technology_Work.pdf

[2]https://www.strategyand.pwc.com/media/file/Strategyand_ Cultures-Role-in-Enabling-Organizational-Change.pdf

## About Claire Croft

For over 20 years, Claire's career has been about inspiring positive behaviour change in people. Before becoming an Executive Coach, she worked within advertising agencies at board level for several years.

Six years ago Claire made the transition into talent development, working in senior roles within two of London's top agencies (*Proximity London* and *M&C Saatchi*) before launching her own highly regarded coaching practice and becoming director of organisational performance consultancy, *Corporate Punk*.

She specialises in helping senior business leaders to unlock both their own potential and that of their employees. Claire is proud to have worked for a broad range of businesses including *Unipart, BBC, Virgin Management* and *Ada*.

*https://corporatepunk.com/*

*https://www.linkedin.com/company/corporate-punk-limited/*

*http://linkedin.com/in/clairelcroft*

# No Leader Is An Island

## Diana Barnett

*No man is an island, entire of itself; every man is a piece
of the Continent, a part of the main ...*

John Donne, poet, 1624.

Sometimes leadership can feel as isolating as living on a desert island and yet as a leader, you are an integral piece of your organisation.

A theory exists that leaders should step out of the system to *work on the business*, yet embracing this concept while juggling the day-to-day grittiness can be challenging for any leader.

If you sometimes feel the isolation of leading an organisation, and the challenges with straddling the working *in* and *on* the business, you may find it beneficial to join a peer-to-peer advisory board, sounding board, think-tank or Mastermind. While these groups have different names and features, fundamentally they all offer the benefits derived from drawing on the experience and different perspectives of fellow leaders.

Another thread is that these groups are a community of peers with a common purpose; through camaraderie they support, question and hold one another accountable to cultivate growth and to impact at both a business and personal level.

## Solid foundations

Masterminds are based on a foundation of trust, honesty and confidentiality.

However, for a Mastermind to flourish and create a micro-climate for growth and to impact each member, the process also requires a willingness of each member to:

- Actively listen
- Give to get
- Ask insightful questions
- Call out the elephant in the room
- Focus on what *can* and *will* be done
- Be accountable

I want to draw on the metaphor/analogy that a Mastermind is like a forest. We have much to learn from nature.

Wired into every tree is the objective to grow to its full potential, and it will do everything in its power to achieve this. Much to the annoyance of humans, a tree's roots spread out to source nutrients and water anywhere they can.

Research has shown that the healthiest forests communicate, share and nurture diversity. While the trees in a forest operate as a group of self-interested individuals, at the same time they will sustain the community. They understand that if as individuals they are to survive, thrive and mature to full capacity, they will benefit by supporting one another. To this end they use those spreading root systems, along with the biome and the wind to communicate with one another.

A tree standing in isolation is less likely to reach its full potential than one that has the support of a community, a forest.

## A community of peers

Like forests, a Mastermind is a community of peers who have individual goals and share a common purpose. They also create a microclimate that encourages sustainable and regenerative growth for each member of the group: this is one of their advantages.

Admittedly such groups are not for everyone. Where some leaders may see the benefits of committing time and energy to a group, others might prefer to work one-on-one with a coach. Both are powerful options, both have their pros and cons, and many leaders will choose to have a coach and also belong to a Mastermind.

My friend Sam, an owner of a successful and substantial business, is a huge fan of the concept of Mastermind, but also works with a coach. He attributes most of his success to his peer group. "Sometimes issues arise that you can't discuss with your management team, your partner, or your best mate and that's why I joined my Mastermind," Sam explains. "It allows me to observe how others have tackled issues and enables me to see the world from diverse and objective perspectives." He adds that – unexpectedly – the best *aha* moments have come from a member in an unrelated industry.

## Collective wisdom and expertise

Masterminds have the benefit of drawing on the collective wisdom and expertise in different contexts and overlaying the angle with a new lens. It's literally stepping out and away to gain clarity.

If you feel Masterminds might be worth exploring, here are some tips and questions to help you find the right group. Proper consideration is critical, given the level of time and energy you'll be committing to your group.

Your first step is to identify the business and personal reasons driving you to join a group, for example:

- Connecting with peers who are driven by a similar purpose
- Having your business scrutinised from a different perspective without bias
- Gleaning insights from across industries
- Leverage the experience, errors and wins of your peers
- Training and development

## As a member of the group are you willing to:

- Be accountable to your peers?
- Be generous with your time, attention and support for other members?
- Share honestly and openly?
- Create and frame a space that holds each member so they feel safe and will share?

## When it's your turn to sit in the hot seat, are you prepared to:

- Acknowledge that personal and business issues will arise in the meeting and will be addressed without judgement?
- Hear someone call out the elephant in the room and ask you insightful questions?
- Actively listen to what is being said without interruption or justification?
- Be fully present and attentive? Allow the richness of time to absorb and reflect on the conversation. It's a powerful way to learn.

- Step away from your industry norms and extrapolate the experience of other industries to your business?

## Assessing the group:

- How was this group curated? Are you aligned with its purpose and values?
- What is the depth and breadth of expertise and experience in the room? Are the member organisations at the same stage of the lifecycle? Does this matter? Can you look beyond the kudos associated with position titles, an organisation's size and the age of the members? What do you bring?
  (Don't undervalue what you bring to the table!)
- What protocols and practices are in place to ensure the meetings run effectively and on time.

Group sizes vary from four to 12 members plus a facilitator. The ideal size of a group will depend on several factors:

- How often you meet
- The length of the meeting
- Where you meet

Finally, and most importantly:

- Are you prepared to drive and inculcate change into your organisation, in the full knowledge that stakeholders often resist change, the unknown and creating new habits?

### SIDEBAR: Start your own group

If you can't find a group that's the right fit, one option is to create a new group from scratch. Key points to consider here are how you'll recruit members, who will facilitate the meetings, and who will attend to the administration that supports the group.

My bias is towards an independent facilitator to hold the space, create safety for each member, manage the time, and to ensure the time is shared equitably. This enables each member to focus on being part of the meeting rather than guiding the process. Alternatively, each member rotate the facilitator role meeting-by-meeting.

## SIDEBAR: Inside a meeting

There is no typical format as each Mastermind will have its own meeting format.

Some groups will meet weekly, fortnightly, monthly or even quarterly. The meetings may run for two hours, or for half a day starting with lunch, while others will run over a three-day weekend retreat. Some groups will combine half-yearly intensive retreats with fortnightly meetings.

Other variables are where the group meets: whether in person, or virtually using online conferencing technology; the number of members in a group; whether the Mastermind is part of a larger organisation; whether it includes professional development and training.

While the logistics of where and when the meeting is held may differ from meeting to meeting, the essence of a meeting is the same, and many agenda will reflect this.

It is ideal to have both a soft and hard start time.

The soft start time enables members to build rapport as they transition from their busy world into the meeting: the social conversation, updates and connections enable members to become present and ready for the hard start.

Then the meeting starts officially with an introduction to the purpose and intention of the meeting: this the hard start.

A good meeting begins and ends on time, paying respect to the members, their time and their other commitments.

The skeleton of most meeting agendas will include a round of:

- Wins and general updates: personal, professional and business.
- Goal accountability: updating achievements from the last meeting.
- Hot seats: each member has the chance to bring an issue or opportunity to the table, framing their session with either *How can I/What can I....*

  The peers then probe for clarification by asking 'insightful questions' before sharing their experience and observations.

  Some groups ban the use of *why...* and *should* as these words may negatively impact the dynamics and interactions of the members. *Why* often puts the person into a defensive mode and *should* is a form of *advice* and may create an imbalance of perceived power.
- Goal setting for the next meeting.
- Completion/wrap up.
- Longer meetings may also include meal breaks, networking, training and team-building exercises

Finally, I want to stress the importance of building into your framework a process for regularly celebrating the milestones and wins of your peers and demonstrating gratitude for their contribution to your growth and development.

*"No two minds ever come together without, thereby, creating a third,invisible, intangible force, which may be likened to a third mind."*

**Napoleon Hill** 1937

Acknowledgement and gratitude for *The Chatham House Rule*. When a meeting, or part thereof, is held under the *Chatham House Rule*, participants are free to use the information received, but neither the identity nor the affiliation of the speaker(s), nor that of any other participant, may be revealed.

- Bungay Stanier. M. (2016). *The Coaching Habit: Say Less, Ask More & Change the Way You Lead Forever.* Box of Crayons
- Hill. N., (1937) *Think and Grow Rich.*
- Hunter. D., Thorpe. S., Brown. H. & Bailey. A. (2009) *The Art of Facilitation: The Essentials for Leading Great Meetings and Creating Group Synergy*, Revised Edition, Jossey-Bass
- Wohlleben. P. (2018) *The Hidden Life of Trees - The Illustrated Edition*, Greystone Book.

## About Diana Barnett

An experienced Mastermind facilitator, Diana Barnett is inspired by leaders who choose regenerative practices to run their businesses for positive social and environmental impact and profit.

Passionate about mining and utilising the collective wisdom and support of peers, she draws on her facilitation training, a deep understanding of people and our connection to the planet to facilitate her Mastermind groups.

Underpinning all Diana's work is her mission to encourage urban-based entrepreneurs to nurture their wellbeing by connecting with nature and using accessible urban green spaces daily.

*LinkedIn https://www.linkedin.com/in/dianabarnettcultiv8/*

*instagram @ https://www.instagram.com/cultiv8impact/*

*Twitter https://twitter.com/Cultiv8Biz*

# What Does it Take for a Family to Survive Financially Over Multiple Generations?

## Nicholas Charles FCCA

Imagine spending all your life working in order to build a business and accumulate wealth that should, by right, establish your legacy and family name. Yet, by the time your grandchildren come of age, the wealth that you worked so hard to establish has completely GONE!

Sadly, this is the reality that is faced by more than ninety percent of all families globally!

The saying, *shirtsleeves to shirtsleeves within three generations*, is actually a reality that is faced by families today. What is more worrying, is that the amount of money is immaterial.

Cornelius Vanderbilt is a classic example of this.

When he passed away in 1877, at the age eighty-two, he left a fortune of $215 billion (2016 dollars, inflation-adjusted[1]). Despite this huge fortune, it took only seventy years for the first bankruptcy to be declared within the family, and in 1973 when the Vanderbilt had a family reunion, there was not a single millionaire among them.

---

1 Gus Lubin, business insider *The 20 Richest People Of All Time*, 2 September 2010

*"It has left me with nothing to hope for, with nothing definite to seek or strive for. Inherited wealth is a real handicap to happiness. It is a certain death to ambition as cocaine is to morality."*

**William K Vanderbilt**, grandson of the self-made Cornelius.

## How Money Flows Within Families

Historical studies have proven that seventy percent of families will lose all their wealth within just two generations, and more than ninety percent of families will lose it within three generations.

This fact was further highlighted by the *2014 Forbes Billionaires List* which revealed that; of the 483 families, less than ten percent were third generation!

This distinct pattern can be highlighted as follows:

- **First Generation (Create the Wealth)** - The emphasis starts with learning how to create wealth, then shifts to creating and growing the wealth-generating business engine and managing cost concerns.

- **Second Generation (Save the Wealth)** – Of the thirty percent that successfully retain the wealth; this generation focuses on growing the business and investing further, so that hopefully, wealth creates further wealth.

- **Third Generation (Spend the Wealth)** – Wealth is received and spent by this generation; who do not hold a meaningful sense of responsibility for wealth management. In this generation, there is no appreciation for wealth or money, other than spending it.

The diagram below perfectly summarises this sad statistic:

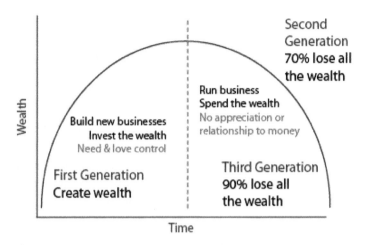

The evidence is therefore clear, from history, and from current research and in practice – seventy percent of families will lose all their wealth within two generations, and over ninety per cent will lose their wealth within just three generations.

So, what can families do, and what actions must they take in order to avoid becoming another damning statistic? More importantly, who within the family should be taking the responsibility to lead the family towards their desired collective vision?

The biggest mistake that any family can make, is to believe that they are above the research and history. Underestimating the likelihood of a disaster and its possible effects, is known as the *normality bias*. This is a belief or mental state, based on the false premise that things will always function the way things have normally functioned. However, can one truly believe that just because everything is going well today, that everything will be fine tomorrow?

How many companies have we seen in the past go bankrupt,

all because they believed in their own hype, and failed to adapt to changing markets or simply thought they were too big to fail? Why should families believe that they are any different?

## Understanding The REAL Problem

It is essential for the family to firstly understand what the problem is, then to obtain clarity on their ideal outcome, before they seek a solution. Unfortunately, families are too quick to outsource, what they believe the problem to be, to professional advisors. Areas such as tax planning, estate planning and financial planning are valuable and should not be dismissed, however, they do not address the real underlying causes of multi-generational financial failure.

The *Williams Group* conducted the most detailed study on the subject of family wealth, and highlighted the real reasons why families lose all their wealth:

60% Poor communication and lack of trust

25% Failure to prepare heirs

10% No family vision

5% Other

The most worrying aspect of this research shows, that even today, very few families know or even appreciate what causes multi-generational failure. Only five percent of families have lost their money because of poor taxation, financial and legal planning, yet the majority, if not all professional advisors focus their expertise within these areas.

The message is therefore clear, effective family leadership is crucial to take pro-active measures to ensure the sustainability of the family dynamic. This extends beyond safeguarding the financial wealth of the family; it's about securing the family legacy by establishing healthy, long-term relationships through effective communication and creating a purpose for the wealth, which is greater than the individual desires of each family member.

Successful, long standing families such as the Rockefeller's and the Rothschild's, have used their vast wealth to make a significant impact on the world through their generous philanthropic ventures which can be measured in the billions of dollars. They have understood that a successful family, much like a successful business, demands strong leadership and a clear, purposeful vision which is shared by all family members.Moreimportantly,theyappreciatethatwealthisnotjust simply measured in terms of financial capital, but also includes the human and intellectual capital - the story and knowledge behind the money. They safeguard the multi-generational success of their family by passing all the wealth on, and not just the financial wealth. By doing so, they demonstrate strong, effective leadership qualities that all families need to follow.

Statistics, research and history all suggest that families, irrespective of how much financial wealth they have, are all fighting an uphill battle for survival. Seventy percent of families will lose their wealth within just two generations, whilst over ninety percent will lose their wealth within just three generations. If one is serious about establishing a long-lasting family legacy and wants to avoid the implosion of the family relationship; a strong, pro-active leadership is a necessity and not an option.

Prevention is better, and significantly cheaper (both emotionally and financially) than a cure. So, why are families not taking the right action required? Maybe it is the inherent fear of *talking about the elephant in the room*, such as openly communicating one's estate with all your family members…

Maybe it is the arrogance that comes with having vast wealth…

Maybe it's the lack of understanding, or even appreciating how big the problem truly is…

Maybe it's as simple as blindly trusting the existing advisors to keep the family and its assets together…

The answer to this question is not obvious, however, the problem is very real.

As a family, if you do not know where you are in terms of assessing the real risks to the family and where you want to go, with a clear family vision, then how can you possibly expect to get the best suited advice? Professional advisors are bound by the instructions of their clients. They may be the best in their field of expertise, but they cannot be expected to understand or appreciate the family dynamics, better than the family itself! To put this into perspective, would anyone simply visit their doctor and ask to be cured without even communicating their symptoms? Of course not, but why are families taking such unnecessary risks and simply *hoping for the best?*

Therefore, only the families with strong leadership that encourage effective communication within the family, set out a vision which inspires all family members and create formal governance structures, are the families that not only survive, but thrive over multiple generations.

*"It requires a great deal of boldness and a great deal of caution to make a great fortune; and when you have got it, it requires ten times more wit to keep it."*

**Nathan Rothschild**

## About Nicholas Charles FCCA

Nicholas Charles FCCA is a family prosperity advisor. He created the *Four Fundamentals* a bespoke programme that helps families to retain their wealth for multiple generations.

In 2009 he was recognised as a *Fellow Chartered Certified Accountant.* Nicholas specialises in family prosperity advice, tax planning, asset protection and property consultancy.

He is the CEO of the *Charles Group* an organisation that bridges the gap between high net worth families and their advisors. Whilst working with families to help them establish and build the *Four Fundamentals* he focuses on the one key area and the foundation for family prosperity – enhanced, effective communication both within the family and externally with their advisors.

He runs his own successful accountancy practice specialising in property tax and looks after a portfolio of high net worth property investors and developers.

Nicholas also runs a multi-million-pound property portfolio. He took over the family portfolio when it had a market value of £4m.

Today that value has quadrupled in asset value along with the rental income.

*FamilyProsperity@CharlesGroup.co.uk*
*Website: www.FamilyProsperity.co.uk*
*Phone: (+44) 20 7263 3295*

# How To Be A Real Leader

## Laura Piccardi

In my experience as a stress management expert and personal performance coach, there are two ends of the leadership spectrum: the *real leader* and the *surface level leader*. On the face of it both are very successful, known for being exceptional at what they do and incredibly driven, but underneath lies a whole different story:

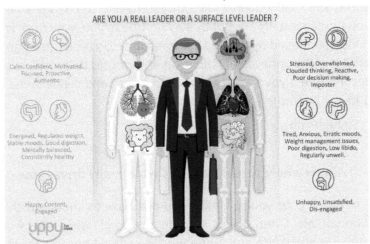

ARE YOU A REAL LEADER OR A SURFACE LEVEL LEADER ?

Calm, Confident, Motivated, Focused, Proactive, Authentic

Energised, Regulated weight, Stable moods, Good digestion, Mentally balanced, Consistently healthy

Happy, Content, Engaged

Stressed, Overwhelmed, Clouded thinking, Reactive, Poor decision making, Imposter

Tired, Anxious, Erratic moods, Weight management issues, Poor digestion, Low libido, Regularly unwell.

Unhappy, Unsatisfied, Dis-engaged

uppy

Now, while it is of course not possible to change the workload, deadlines and pressure that inevitably come with leadership, it is possible to change the way you respond to it. You have much more control over the way you experience the world than you might think, and once you can master this control you have the power to create whatever responses and experiences you want, and therefore move up to the real leader end of the spectrum. What that means is, you can experience less stress, less overwhelm, less frustration and less worry, meaning your body and brain can remain more calm, energised and well, and you can operate with more confidence, focus, clarity and purpose. As I'm sure you can appreciate, the impact of that is exponential on your ability to lead and perform both professionally and personally.

Let me explain all of this in more detail, by outlining to you the three key areas that must be addressed in order to achieve this control. Before I get onto the specifics however, it's important to highlight the ultimate outcome we're striving for here – and that is for you to be able to show up as yourself 100% without restrictions at all times. Of course you may have to adapt your delivery and manner to suit a person and situation, but that's just surface level stuff in order to create the right environment, and is still totally doable without you having to change who you fundamentally are. But by staying true to you, your drive is no longer fuelled by a need to prove yourself, so you can let go of a lot of the unnecessary thoughts and worries that make you second guess yourself, question your worth and create stress, and just be free to focus on what matters.

So here's how you can get that.

## 1. Know who you really are and what really drives you

In order to be yourself 100% you first have to know exactly who you are. Often we get stuck in a cycle of doing what we think we *should* do and being who we *should* be, as a result of our fundamental lack of belief in our worth and the many influences that surround us every day, such as our colleagues, friends, family, competitors, the media, and social norms and expectations. We subconsciously compare ourselves to what's going on around us and try to adapt to *fit in* and avoid being rejected.

As a result we don't feel fulfilled because we're not working on the things that really matter to us, and we feel like life is just taking us along for the ride rather than us being in the driver's seat. So we try to fill the void and ensure we don't get found out as the fraud we think we are by working harder for longer and seeking external gratification. Of course this then pushes us further into the stress cycle until eventually something has to give – our health, relationships and even sometimes our life.

By taking the time to uncover and intimately understand your personal core values and what you truly want in all areas of your life, you have what I call your *life blueprint*, which becomes your guide for everything you do – whether that's making a decision, choosing a path or simply knowing how to make yourself feel good at any given time. If you're living by your values and consistently taking action towards what you really want, that's when you show up as yourself and achieve true balance – because your external behaviours are in alignment with your internal drivers.

## 2. Understand and respect the connection between the mind and body

When you're constantly on the go and never switching off your brain thinks you're in danger so it puts your body into fight or flight mode to ensure you survive.

Here's the thing, even though the world has evolved at an amazing rate, your brain has not. The brain doesn't know the difference between real and perceived danger, so even though the *danger* nowadays is simply thoughts and worries, it still responds in the same way it did right back in prehistoric times when a sabre tooth tiger was chasing you – it activates the sympathetic nervous system and sets off a series of physiological processes to ensure you can stand up for yourself or get the hell out of there.

Now, because you're not actually fighting or running away, these physiological processes are not being utilised so they start to wreak havoc in your body. Important processes like digestion, hormone regulation, weight management and brain function become dysfunctional, so your risk of sickness and disease increases, energy levels, mood and motivation become erratic and your ability to make decisions and be proactive declines. Can you believe that all of this can come as a result of a simple interpretation by your brain that something is stressful and therefore poses a threat to you?

In the next point we'll look at how you can take more control of these interpretations, but for now let's talk about some physical strategies you can employ to calm your body and reduce the amount of time you're in fight or flight mode. The main principal to remember is to communicate to your brain as often as you can that you're safe. This triggers your parasympathetic nervous system (or rest and digest mode) to come into play. As I said before, you can't take away all of the stressors, but you can balance them out so their impact is minimal. So, anything you can do that is basically the opposite of fighting or running away is the aim of the game.

**Breathing slowly and deeply** is a perfect example – the brain knows that if you're able to control your breathing then danger can't be present, because if it was you'd be physically protecting yourself so breathing fast and shallow. You can of course supersize this with meditation, and reap further benefits such as improved cognitive function.

**Doing something you love** is also a great way to communicate safety because when you're having a good time you feel secure and content at your core, which is most definitely not the feeling you have when you're stressed and in danger.

This could be something as simple as popping your headphones in and listening to a favourite song, watching a video of puppies on *YouTube*, or giving your best mate a call. Check in with your values here and they will guide you on what to do.

As you can see, the strategies to physically calm your body down are not difficult, but the key is consistency.

By scheduling these activities into you diary throughout the day every day, you'll build up your bank of calm so you'll naturally start to respond differently anyway.

### 3. Master the way you communicate with yourself

You are absolutely what you think. The brain wants your internal and external worlds to be aligned, so it will organise all the information you absorb to determine how you interpret and experience the external world, based on what's going on internally inside your mind – your thoughts, experiences, beliefs, values, memories and attitudes.

A really simple example of this is when you buy a new car, and then you start to see that car everywhere you go – have you had that? It's not that there are suddenly more of those cars on the road, it's that you have the image of the car imprinted in your mind so your brain is seeking to align that with what you consciously see in the external world.

If you can identify and focus on those elements of your mind that align most with who you really are and what you really want, and change those that don't, you can take control of how you interpret the world and therefore take control of how you respond and how you experience it.

Let's say, for example, you have a core belief that you're not good enough (the majority of people do to some degree). Because this belief is present in your internal world, your brain will interpret interactions and situations in your external world that align with this belief. So, if you're constantly validating the fact that you're not good enough, this of course is going to drive your need to prove yourself and cause you to work harder, create more pressure and trigger the stress response.

On the flip side, if you're constantly communicating to yourself internally that you are good enough, you're living according to your values and you seek the learnings in everything, can you see how your external interpretations could be very different? You'll no longer feel like you need to compensate for not being good enough, you'll see more opportunities that align with who you really are and what's really important to you, and you'll approach situations with your problem solving and logical mind ... therefore less unnecessary pressure and less stress.

So really, the most important thing in terms of being a real leader in all areas of your life is this last point of mastering the way you communicate with yourself. Of course, knowing who you are and what you want allows you to determine what you need to communicate, but since all things start in your mind – from your physical health to the way you feel and experience the world – focusing on this is most definitely what will give you the greatest return on your time and efforts.

## About Laura Piccardi

Laura is an International Stress Management Expert, Performance Coach, Speaker and Author of the bestselling book, *Unfaked*. Her mission is to make a massive dent in the statistics of lifestyle related disease and levels of distress, that are rapidly increasing as a result of our highly pressured and busy lifestyles.

Laura's incredible story of transforming her own life, after she worked herself into the ground and watched her business burn down, is the inspiration behind her mission. She recognised that while people now have more opportunities than ever, they are also more stressed out and overwhelmed than ever, which is impacting their health, relationships and mental wellbeing.

Laura's journey and experience working with hundreds of clients allowed her to create a methodology, that she now uses to teach others how to change the way they think and behave, so they too can live truly healthy and fulfilled lives.

The results are life changing.

*Website: https://uppy.com.au/*

*Book: https://uppy.com.au/unfaked-2/*

*LinkedIn: https://www.linkedin.com/in/laura-piccardi-uppy/*

*Facebook: https://www.facebook.com/liveuppy/*

# Be Ollin

## Errol Lawson

When an earthquake or great storm shook the earth, the ancient Aztecs described such power with a single word: *Ollin*.

It is a word that can be found on the Aztec calendar and on many of the instruments used in sacred pre-Columbian ceremonies. Pronounced *ALL-in*, it's an expression of immense depth that conveys intense and immediate movement.

Stemming from the ancient Nahuatl language, *Ollin* is derived from *yollotl*, meaning heart, and *yolistli*, meaning life. *Ollin* means to move and act now with all your heart. It means to follow your path in life wholeheartedly. To experience *Ollin* we have to get *All-in*. Especially as leaders.

When an earthquake occurs, it signals it's now time to move and act with full purpose of heart.

### The power of being Ollin

Being *Ollin* is essential to effective self - leadership. For us to grow and to make the gains that we are looking for we need to be *Ollin*. As leaders we set the standard for the level of commitment and passion that we want to see from those in our teams. The culture of our organisations is determined largely by the attitude, behaviour and beliefs that we demonstrate.

The Aztecs envisioned wearing your heart on your face to allow your eyes to open and see more clearly. When we view our path with clarity, we move with accelerated purpose and intent. We go forward with a full and committed heart.

The Aztecs called it an *Ollin* heart.

They believed that everyone had a sacred path that led to their life's purpose. It was up to each individual to discover what they needed to do in their life and then give it their all. They believed that if everyone could find their purpose, the thing that made their hearts beat fast, the entire society could find its *Ollin*. It was not just an individual endeavor. It was a communal endeavor.

I first came across the word *Ollin* back in 2010 when I read Kevin Hall's book *Aspire: Discovering your Purpose through the Power of Words,* and a book I highly recommend. The word made such a profound impact because for me it summed up the what life is really about in one simple word. It speaks about what it takes for both individual and collective progress and transformation to happen. Kevin says:

> *"The words Ollin and passion are two sides of the same coin. They are companions, inexorably intertwined. Together, they produce enormous results. When we decide what it is we are willing to suffer for, and what we are equally willing to act on, the world opens up."*

This is why I've started this journey with you by talking about the need for us to be *Ollin*.

## What does it mean to be *Ollin*?

To me *Ollin* means lots of things. It means to burn the boats. Nearly five years ago, I was facing an important decision, a crossroads in my church ministry that, depending on its outcome, would greatly impact my future. I had spent the past ten years serving in my local church, as a youth pastor, operations manager and many other roles. I was leaving my post and debating whether to seek another similar post in an existing church or to build a team and start a brand new church. I left both doors open for a while before committing firmly to the latter. I put my stake in the ground and got to work.

The first year was tough. Compounding the fact that I was single, (and wanting to marry) trying to build credibility, build a team and make meaningful connections in a new field, I was also dealing with moving house. As you can imagine, my phone wasn't exactly ringing off during the first few months. But even then, when I didn't know how I was going to pay my bills, I had no regrets. I was committed to my new direction and had burned my boats. There was no looking back.

The concept of burning boats traces back to one of history's most inspiring leadership stories in 1519. Hernán Cortés led a large expedition consisting of 600 Spaniards, 16 or so horses, and 11 boats to Mexico. The goal: capture a magnificent treasure said to be held there. Upon arrival, Cortés made history by destroying his ships. This sent a clear message to his men: *There is no turning back.* They either win or they perish.

Although you might assume that Cortés' men would have become despondent, with no exit strategy in place to save their lives, they instead rallied behind their leader as never before. Within two years, he succeeded in his conquest of the Aztec empire. (Some date this concept even further back in history, to the times of Julius Caesar—in his conquest of England— or even the Ancient Greeks. Regardless, the scenarios and impact were similar.)

To be *Ollin*, remember pronounced *ALL IN*, you have to learn to make a decision and commit to seeing it through. To put all your energy, heart and focus into what it is that you are attempting to achieve. It can be like taking a leap of faith, stepping into the unknown with a total determination and commitment to see it through.

To be *Ollin* means to confront and push back the doubts and fears that can some time get in the way. Those negative and limiting voices in our heads or coming from those around us that can cause us to question ourselves and our capability.

To be *Ollin* means to show up. To be present. To not just be in the room but to let your light shine in the room, in the conversation, wherever you go. To be intentional about making a positive contribution in whatever you are involved with.

To be *Ollin* is to be prepared. That means that whenever you show up for anything you are ready. You have done your homework. You have prepared what you are going to do or say, you are ready. You deliver the best possible results because you are prepared to do so. Not by accident.

To be *Ollin* means to lay aside every weight and distraction that can be holding us back. In *Hebrews* Chapter 12, the Apostle Paul writes to the Hebrews instructing them to *let us strip off every weight that slows us down, especially the sin that so easily trips us up. And let us run with endurance the race God has set before us.*

We have to let go of some stuff in order to be *Ollin*. The level of thinking, the habits and behaviours that got us to this point are not going to be sufficient for us to be able to finish our journey well.

To be *Ollin* means to pursue your goal with blinkers on. Totally focussed on what lays ahead.

No looking back.

### What are the consequences of *not* being *Ollin*?

There is a cost of not being *Ollin*. The area I struggle most to be *Ollin* is with my exercise and nutrition. As I am writing this I am renewing my commitment to get *Ollin* again in this area. The reality is that although my levels of commitment have improved in the last 2-3 years I have been up and down. Training hard one month and eating well. Then not training for a few weeks and letting my diet slip and then getting back on it again. It's a little discouraging to be honest. I know I can and should do better than I am doing and I haven't been respecting my body.

This is the consequence of not being *Ollin*. If we are not careful we can go through life feeling permanently dissatisfied. Always in a state of *shoulda woulda coulda* and never actually getting anything done.

If we don't get *Ollin* we will never know how great we could become and risk living life with regrets.

If we don't get *Ollin* we have to live with what I call *Almost there syndrome*. Where we always get *so close*, we can see the light at the end of the tunnel, but we never quite make it. We never experience the joy and fulfilment of reaching the goal.

If we don't get *Ollin* we can condemn ourselves to an average life with average results.

People who are not *Ollin* will always find themselves as an employee or a subject of those that are *Ollin*.

When you're not *Ollin* you can very easily fall into the comparison trap where you find yourself looking around at others wishing you had what they had.

## What are the benefits of being *Ollin*?

The areas of my life were I am most *Ollin* are my faith and my family. Nothing comes close. My wife and my two daughters are the world to me. They bring me so much joy. I am totally committed to them and not just in word but in deed. I make sure I carve out as much time as possible for us to spend quality time together and to learn, grow and play together. I have built a business that allows me to be able to provide for them and to give them a great quality of life.

When it comes to family I'm *Ollin*.

Since becoming a Christian in 2004, I have grown in my commitment to being *Ollin* and I am still growing.

For me being *Ollin* as a Christian means to surrender my whole life to Christ. Like, if I am going to make Jesus Lord of my life it has to be every area of my life. When I was younger in my faith I'd say, *Jesus you can be my Lord but I'll control my finances,* or *I'll control my relationships* or *you can be my Lord on Sunday but I'll control Monday to Saturday.*

Being *Ollin* means that He is Lord of *every* area of my life, *every* day of the week. Being *Ollin* brings:

- Increased focus
- Increased passion
- Increased growth
- You learn great lessons from life along the way that you perhaps wouldn't otherwise learn.
- You get to inspire others with your own faith and courage
- You become a respected and influential leader among your peers and community
- You start to experience great results in your work
- You begin to discover and fulfil your purpose
- You start to make a difference in the world and in the lives of those around you

- You live a fulfilled life
- You become a magnet for opportunities
- Doors of opportunities begin to open up to you

## Steps to take to become *Ollin*

Hopefully you can get a sense of how being *Ollin* vs not being *Ollin* can make a big difference to your life. Firstly, you have to be honest with yourself about the areas that you are not *Ollin* right now and about the damage it is doing to you physically, psychologically or otherwise.

I mentioned in my earlier example that I went through a time when I was at a crossroads in my ministry journey. Unsure about what step to take. I left my options open for a while before taking a decision. Sometimes you have to do that. You have to wait. Not waiting and doing nothing though, actively waiting. While waiting I was in prayer and fasting to God about which direction to take. I was speaking to other experienced people that had more life and church leadership experience and hearing their advice. I was preparing myself mentally and emotionally for the journey ahead. Attended courses and conferences, reading books. All in preparation for the next step. You might night feel like you can be *Ollin* but you can.

Firstly, you have to be honest with yourself about he areas that you are not *Ollin* right now and about the damage it is doing to you physically, psychologically or otherwise.

If you're someone that has a faith in God I highly recommend the you pray about the areas of your life in which you want to be *Ollin*. Talk to God about it in all humility.

Make a list of the bad habits and behaviours that are holding you back and start to drop them off one by one.

Make yourself accountable to a friend or a group of people that can help you and that will check in on your progress. Not just anyone but someone you value and respect. When we are accountable to others we tend to raise our game and get things done. When we lack accountability we tend to procrastinate and put things off until tomorrow. And tomorrow never comes.

Take action. What does action look like. It likes as soon as I finish writing this chapter I am going to do a 30 minute workout and have a healthy breakfast and start my day right. I am going to speak to my wife about my desire to be *Ollin* in the area of my health and fitness. I am going to ensure that our environment is free from the types of food that I like to binge on. I am going to get on the scales and weigh myself, which I haven't done in a while.

In whatever the area of your life it sis that you desire to be *Ollin* do something write now to take action towards it.

And then lastly, measure your results. You may have heard the saying, W*hat gets measured gets done.* It means regular measurement and reporting keeps you focused — because you use that information to make decisions to improve your results.

Your most critical measurements are called *Key Performance Indicators.* So I am going to get on the scales and measure my weight. Where do you need to measure? Is it your time spent with loved ones? You bank balance? Time spent in prayer and meditation? Get measuring.

The key to *Ollin* is self-leadership. The benefits to others are profound.

## About Errol Lawson

Behind the grin is a compelling story of misspent youth when Errol's life was ruled by gangs, crime and drugs. Not only did he claw his way back to the right side, Errol has gone on to become a successful entrepreneur, author, ordained minister and sought-after motivational speaker.

Through his company *Emerge Leadership UK*, Errol is known for developing leaders that are positively transforming communities around the world. Errol is a case study in personal responsibility. Errol and his wife lead *The Bridge Church*, an *Assemblies of God* church in Harborne in Birmingham.

Errol is also the best-selling author of *From the Postcode to the Globe - How to overcome limitations and realise your potential,* and *Teenpreneur - How to build a business in your teens.*

Outside of work Errol is the doting dad of two little girls with his superpowers bolstered by making the *Birmingham Post's Power 250* list as *One of the most powerful and influential people in the Midlands.*

*(+44) 7852397747*

*errol@errollawson.com*

*www.errollawson.com*

*www.emerge-leadership.com*

*Twitter @errollawson*

# Plan For Purpose And Financial Success

## Jason Graystone

It's no secret that financial wellbeing is an important part of life.

In fact, after oxygen and water, it's one of the most important elements we need to survive. Having money can literally mean the difference between life and death.

Furthermore, it is one of the biggest contributors to your quality of lifestyle, and it is a massive determinate of how you spend your time on earth.

Having said that, building financial wealth is not the only thing to set goals for in life.

There are 6 other key areas of personal development that will ultimately determine your empowerment and fulfilment:

- Health/Fitness
- Business/Vocation
- Self Development/Knowledge
- Relationships/Partnerships
- Social Leadership
- Spirituality

These other areas should also not be ignored.

Money can be used to buy the best food, a gym membership, start a business, buy courses, books, masterminds, take your partner on a date, reach a broader demographic with your message and much more.

But most of all, it helps you stay clear about your purpose and remain on mission whilst chaos and disorder happens around you.

People commonly assume that if they win the lottery, or somehow fall into a lot of money, that it will solve all of their problems in all areas of life. This is simply not true and can be a deadly mental trap to fall into.

As many would agree, being poor and healthy is likely more desirable than being a millionaire on his deathbed, unready to leave this earth.

But I believe that financial wellbeing filters down into all other areas of life, but it's all about balance.

I often get told by people with a low value on financial independence that *money isn't important* or *money doesn't make you happy.* This is only a partial truth.

I've also been told *we don't need money, we have a happy relationship without it.* Again, this is just one important area of life that is a separate study to money.

If money is used correctly, as a tool, it can not only be used to enhance all other areas of your life, but it can be used to empower your purpose.

So, why don't we? Well it's mainly down to planning.

We see money used as a reactive tool instead of a proactive tool.

We all take precautions such as insuring our homes because we know that should we have a flood, fire or be the victim of theft, we are protected to some degree and the thought of the pain we would go through should we not be protected from such events makes it a no-brainer to pay to keep our homes insured.

We plan for outcomes. But people treat money as a *get out of jail* instead of a *not go to jail* tool.

In this example, it's like having no home insurance, suffering a flood in your home, and then ringing the insurer after the event to get insurance. It's too late.

Money also has a much greater benefit than the fair exchange tool it was designed for. It keeps us calm.

An ordered mind is capable of dealing with more complexity in the real world. The more simplistic our minds are, the more complexity we can deal with.

When we have broad time and space horizons in our mind, we are able to focus on meaningful and inspiring work.

Instead of seeing day to day, we see years, decades, or even centuries ahead.

We are able to be better leaders when we have clarity over decisions and actions based on our ability to see further ahead than our own nose.

Money plays a big part in allowing us to see a bigger picture and play a bigger game.

All we have to do is plan. Whatever we plan, we achieve.

If you have ever planned a holiday, the holiday has gone to plan. If you have ever planned a party, the chances are, the party happened. If you have ever planned a barbeque, it took place.

The reason they successfully take place is because we PLAN them.

Being able to live on purpose is about being free and able to take actions aligned with our values each and every day and plan how we spend our time on the rock.

When we are born, we have certain desires that make us unique.

The people we are attracted to, the food we like, the activities we enjoy, the music we listen to etc.

These are the little flecks of gold that make us who we are.

The reason people lose track of these little flecks of gold is because the actions they take based on influenced decisions they have made have led them down a path they didn't plan for.

Today, we see so many people setting goals, but little effort is put into planning them.

The same goes for their use of money.

They get paid, spend it and have no plan for the future. This results in them feeling the pressure of their expenses and debts as they increase their lifestyle with their income.

By doing this, they are moving further away from their purpose. They think that the more money they earn, the more chance they will have at becoming financially independent, but this is only true if they plan how to use their money.

I know plenty of high income earners who have no time to think about their purpose because they are on a treadmill, turning up the speed every day.

I also know low income earners who have lots of savings and are doing what they love, however, they are stunted in their potential because they haven't planned for financial growth as well as financial accumulation.

So how do we plan?

Well first of all, we must know what the objectives are, then we can plan for each one. We need to be able to master balance in order to do what we love and love what we do.

The objective is to live an inspired life.

## Time Is Money

I believe wealth is measured in time.

We hear people say too often that *time is money*. This is not true. The more you believe this, the more you will charge for your time and be limited by the hours in the day.

In order to live an inspired and purposeful life, we must switch this on its head and ask ourselves, *how much time can we buy into the future?*

The more time you can buy, the freer you feel and the more you can do meaningful work. But I'm not a believer in scrimping and stashing everything you earn because this also results in an uninspired and resentful life.

In order to achieve success in all areas of life, we must first get our money game right by following some key steps:

## The key steps

1. Control your living expenses
2. Save an ever-growing portion of our income each month (purpose account)
3. Invest your money to the market regularly
4. Allocate 10% of your income to self-development (mind account)
5. Spend the rest on your living necessities (body account)
6. Automate your banking so the above steps take place automatically.

This is a basic plan to build wealth and look after all other areas of your life. It's a plan.

If we take our holiday planning example earlier, how long would you say that you spend planning a seven-day holiday?

Looking online at locations, doing price comparisons, booking flights, booking insurance, book airport parking or taxi etc.

I think it's safe to say that we usually spend around two hours booking a holiday that lasts seven days.

If you do the math, this planning equates to 1.8% of the holiday (not including sleep time).

If we apply this to planning our year, it would mean that in order to have a successful year, we would need to spend around 7-10 days planning our year.

Do you spend 7-10 days planning your year? If you did, you would have far more success. Not only in your finances but in ALL areas of life.

## Plan

Print out your bank statement over the last 12 months, sit down and *look at what you are spending each month*. Write a list of all of the outgoings that can be reduced and score it on saving priority.

Add up all of the monthly savings and allocate it to one of the following:

- Savings account
- Books
- Courses
- Masterminds
- Bootcamps

Next, *set up a separate account for your savings* and an

automatic transfer each month instructing your bank to allocate a minimum of 10% of your income to this account.

Set a reminder on your calendar every three months to increase this transfer by an additional 10%. Think of this as paying yourself first, paying your purpose first.

Each time you ramp up your savings, you will feel the pinch. But as the ninety days go by, you will acclimatise to it and you will be ready to put demand on your financial freedom again. Do it!

It will also force you to be creative about growing your income.

This is the next step. *Grow your income by 10% each year.*

This is where planning comes into play. Many people who run their own businesses get lost in the murky water and there is no divide when it comes to balance in the areas of life.

It's important to work on your business but it's also important to maintain important relationships.

I remember when I started trading full time and working from home. It was a challenge.

Before, when I had been going out to work every day and working in an office, I could have stayed out from 06:00 until 22:00 and I would have been considered a hard-working hero.

But when I started disappearing into my home office, I was *ignoring the family.*

My kids and wife didn't know when they could talk to me or when they would ever see me again.

I knew that if I was to be able to work on our financial future, I also had to keep a balance in the home otherwise I would be the millionaire on his deathbed with no one around.

We went to the office suppliers and bought the biggest white board we could find.

On the white board we drew each day of the week and

every hour from 05:00 until 22:00. We took a yellow marker and wrote down all of the non-negotiable family time slots across the week.

- Walks
- Dinner
- Lunch
- Family board game
- Family film
- Child 1 time
- Child 2 time
- Date night
- Hot tub session
- No-Technology time

Once these blocks were set, we then each took a preferred colour marker of our own and then populated the board with our own activities. I blocked in all of the time slots I wanted to work on my business.

The transformation in our family was incredible. Certainty, clarity, reassurance and respect. My kids knew when they could spend time with me. Myself and my wife got excited about regular date nights, my business grew fast as did my income because I had the balance to think creatively and produce my best work.

Everyone wants to live an inspired life.

I believe that when we are free and able to focus on meaningful work, we become better human beings.

I also believe that how we handle and manage our finances dictates whether or not we live out our purpose or not.

If we focus on planning our future, we can be who we want to be and create something meaningful that lasts far beyond our earthly life.

## About Jason Graystone

Since starting his first business at 22 years old, Jason has successfully built and run multi million pound businesses both in the service sector and online. At age 24, Jason found a love for investing.

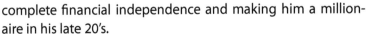

A combination of passive investing and speculation in the financial markets allowed him to adopt a powerful wealth acceleration strategy, helping him achieve complete financial independence and making him a millionaire in his late 20's.

Jason's contribution in the financial education space has been recognised as being radically transparent and transferable.

His refreshingly honest and insightful approach to helping other investors and traders succeed has since been commended by Forbes magazine which he has been featured in for his innovative work towards trader development.

A large part of his trading success was built on a foundation of becoming a business owner first. His obsession with statistics and data is what he believes has led him to discover the missing links in todays trading education.

Jason has a vast global successful trading community made up of serious traders and investors who are part of his training platform.

Jason believes that everyone deserves to live an inspired life. "When we are free and able to focus on our highest values and undertake meaningful work, we become better human beings".

*Jason Graystone Website: http://www.jasongraystone.com*
*Email: info@jasongraystone.com*
*Facebook: http://www.facebook.com/jasongraystone*
*Instagram: http://instagram.com/j_graystone*
*Twitter: http://twitter.com/jasongraystone*
*LinkedIn: http://linkedin.com/in/jasongraystone*
*Podcast: http://bit.ly/alwaysfreepodcast*

# Playing By The Rules

## Andrew Priestley

Who do you admire and respect and would follow as a leader? What is it about them that has your attention? The people I admire, respect *and would follow* have integrity and character.

It's 2004, and it's poolside for the 400m freestyle final heats at the Australian Championships selection qualifier for 2004 *Athens Summer Olympic Games.*

Without a doubt the air is electric. Lining up is champion swimmer, Ian Thorpe - like Mark Spitz and Michael Phelps hydraulically proportioned to dominate the pool.

Appropriately nicknamed *Thorpedo*, Thorpe is already a multi-gold medalist, swimming superstar and national hero. And he has already qualified for the 100m and 200m.

The swimmers assemble and climb the starters blocks. For whatever reason, the unthinkable happens.

He overbalances and falls off the starters block resulting in an instant disqualification from seasoned poolside official, John Keppie. This is an upset of epic proportions.

The decision is appealed by Thorpe's coach. As reported, it is claimed that *Thorpe was kept waiting* and *a noise caused Thorpe to make the error.* The appeal is dismissed by Keppie, ending Thorpe's chance to defend the 400m freestyle Olympic title.

The reaction Australia-wide is instant. Thorpe is Australia's Gold medal hopeful - a surety - and now those hopes are dashed. *There must be a way to get him back in the race.*

What ensues is a media frenzy sparking widespread national debate. The Prime Minister of the day, John Howard, calls it a *tragedy*. Major sporting figures weigh into the debate. They call for the selection policy to be *relaxed*.

The second placed swimmer, 23 year-old Craig Stevens qualifies to defend the 400m and almost immediately there is immense populist pressure to have Stevens, a champion in his own right, step aside and hand his place back to Thorpe.

In the next few days, Stevens announces he will step aside *to concentrate on other events* he has qualified for. It emerges that he was offered $130,000 to become a commentator for the television broadcaster, the *Seven Network* at the Olympics - essentially $325 per metre.

This generates a massive ethical debate - should Stevens have stepped aside for cash? Stevens denies that he was motivated by the money.

In any event, Stevens step aside and Thorpe accepts the gesture.

*Everyone wants ... and gets a fairy tale ending.*

But not everyone sees it that way.

John Keppie, a highly respected veteran swimming official is criticised severely for dashing Australia's chances to win gold.

Keppie says, "*It wasn't a tough call.* We explain to referees coming up that it doesn't matter who is on the blocks, they are just a person. To me, it was just the athlete in lane four who started before the starting signal. It was the only thing I could do, otherwise I would have lost the respect of my colleagues, I would have lost the respect long term of the coaches, the public and everybody else."

"To me, whether it was a 12-year-old or 14-year-old, the rule would have applied."

These are the rules, they won't be bent for anyone.

Keppie is right.

Kieren Perkins, himself an Olympic gold medalist swimming legend, describes the affair as *grubby* and *"a very, very sad tale for Australian sport."*

Perkins is right.

A prominent sports commentator weighing into the debate explains it wonderfully. Paraphrasing:

"Trust me, if you are lining up for an Olympic qualifier, you are no slouch in the pool. Craig Stevens is easily Olympic standard. Everyone on the starters blocks has been there hundreds of times before - *they know the rules*. If you fall off the blocks before the race commences, you get disqualified. Thorpe knew that."

Perkins also reacted strongly to the populist view that *we should waive the rules ... just this once.*

"It sends the wrong message to every kid that aspires to compete."

When asked if the IOC should intervene, Olympic gold medalist Suzie O'Neill says they shouldn't. She reaffirms the view that rules are rules; and that Craig Stevens is a champion in his own right and a medal chance.

O'Niell is asked, "Do you think it devalues that event though, when you know, when the spectators know, and the other swimmers know that the best swimmer in this event isn't actually competing?"

O'Neill is adamant. "As far I'm concerned a gold medal is a gold medal at the Olympics, no matter what sport and who is there, and that's what it's all about."

But what is it all about? It's about fairness and rules and reality. And integrity and character.

Perkins was right. Keppie was right. Those are the rules. We don't cheat. We don't massage the truth. We do not look the other way. We do not win at any cost. We do not expect the rules to be relaxed for us, just this once. We win fairly. We trust in fairness. We accept the good with the bad.

We look up to our national sporting heroes. We value the leadership of people like Kieren Perkins, Dame Kelly Holmes and Sir Chris Hoy because they play a fair game. An honourable game. Win, draw, lose, we trust - rely - on their integrity to stand by the rules and the outcome.

In sport, we denigrate cheats of any kind.

Be very clear, *Ian Thorpe did not cheat*. The public just didn't like the result and wanted to bend the rules. They wanted a champion and he got caught up in that.

But that's not how it should work. Perkins is right. It does send a bad message to kids, and competitors and makes winning meaningless.

The *right thing* looks like leadership.


But we accept that outside of sport. I lost faith in politicians in 1996, when after winning an Australian Federal election John Howard slashed spending to *Education* and *Social Welfare* blaming a budget deficit left by a previous government. When it was pointed out that he had *promised* not to cut spending on these areas as part of his election platform and that he had lied, he claimed that these were *non-core promises*.

A *non-core promise* is a commitment to deliver a service, funding item etc that can be subsequently set aside with a glib excuse.

The problem is, people act in accordance with what they believe to be true.

In 2016, in the UK, we are told, *"We send the EU £350m a week, let's fund our NHS instead"*. This bus slogan is credited with being influential in *Leave EU* winning the vote but has been controversial ever since.

But was that the truth?

If I mislead a customer I can be fined, struck off or go to jail and have my reputation in tatters. But it appears, if I am politician, I can commit gross public mischievousness on a scale that is economically crippling and on far reaching proportions - without consequence.

We look to all leaders to be responsible. To lead honestly. Otherwise, we are complicit in *whatever it takes*. If so, we should accept that whatever follows next, we sanctioned.

I was business mentored by straight shooters.

They understood the concept of being a grown-up where we accept that life and business deals out success and failure and we should take that in our stride. Where we play by the rules, play fairly and do what is for the greater good.

In 2019, sadly, there are few *profiled* political leaders we can admire or respect. Or trust. Or *should* trust.

But I am still a fan of business leaders who in my experience, on the balance play by the rules and use their influence for the greater good. Thankfully, this is an area that continues to inspire me and an arena I wish to leave in better shape.

Thorpe won gold in the 400m freestyle in Athens. Just thought you should know.

It is reported that Thorpe appeared to shed tears in an uncharacteristic sign of emotion, admitting afterwards that the controversy surrounding the event had taken a toll on him, but denying that any *liquid* had left his eyes.

Undeniably, Thorpe was and remains a champion. Michael Phelps claims Thorpe was the *greatest middle-distance swimmer or all time*. Dawn Fraser says Thorpe was the *greatest swimmer in the world*. Watch any of Thorpe's races on *YouTube* and you will see *exactly* what a true champion looks like in the pool.

So I have the utmost respect.

I do not know Thorpe personally, but my hunch from this distance is that the events of 2004 may have been what *appeared* to dull his passion for swimming - and winning - which lead to his subsequent retirement in 2006.

As a business coach specialising in leadership, qualified in psychology, focused on achievement I have had the privilege to peak under the bonnet and into the minds of some very high performers. I can assure you that at that level, integrity is definitely linked to sustained high performance.

I like winners but I am not a fan of doing *whatever it takes* to win. And it comes at a high price, anyway.

Whenever you violate your own integrity and rationalise poor performance, you start to make mistakes in judgement, your performance drops and your game will suffer. And even if everyone *thinks* you are a winner, and outwardly it *looks* like that, in your heart of hearts you know the truth.

When you put your head on the pillow at night, you sleep with you. *You know what happened.*

If you play a straight bat, then even if life goes against you, if you stick to the rules and stay on the right side of the argument, life remains sweet. That is integrity and character. And there's a lot to be said for sleeping easy.

## References

- https://en.wikipedia.org/wiki/Ian_Thorpe_false_start_controversy
- https://www.smh.com.au/sport/swimming/why-I-disqualified-ian-thorpe--swimming-official-opens-up-about-thorpedo-flop-20150725-gikeea.html
- https://www.smh.com.au/sport/its-your-race-ian-at-325-a-metre-20040427-gditd9.html
- http://www.abc.net.au/pm/content/2004/s1076565.htm
- https://www.telegraph.co.uk/politics/2019/05/16/350m-brexit-bus-slogan-lie-says-jean-claude-juncker/
- https://www.urbandictionary.com/define.php?term=non-core%20promise
- https://www.theguardian.com/politics/reality-check/2016/may/23/does-the-eu-really-cost-the-uk-350m-a-week
- https://en.wikipedia.org/wiki/Swimming_at_the_2004_Summer_Olympics_-_Men%27s_400_metre_freestyle

## About Andrew Priestley

Andrew Priestley is a qualified award winning business leadership coach and was ranked in the Top 100 UK Entrepreneur Mentors 2017. He is the best-selling author of three books: *The Money Chimp*, *Starting* and *Awareness*, as well as the editor of multiple expert author books on leadership and on sales. He is an international speaker and the founder MD of *The Coaching Experience*.

He started his business life as the publisher of an lifestyle/entertainment newspaper *Big Night Out* in direct competition with Rupert Murdoch. For the record, Murdoch won!

From there he created a marketing agency and was head hunted to several marketing agencies as an accounts manager.

Andrew went back to university and completed his Industrial and Organisational psychology degree and then became a business coach specialising in applied psychology.

In addition to a multi-award winning high performance executive coaching business he is also the Chairman of Trustees for *Clear Sky Children's Charity UK*, which provides play therapy for children aged 4-12 who have witnessed or directly experienced a trauma. *Clear Sky Children's Charity* was nominated as a charity of the year in 2019.

You can find Andrew on *LinkedIn* or

*www.andrewpriestley.com*

# Would You Like To Contribute To Future Editions Of
## *Fit For Purpose Leadership?*

If you would like to contribute to *Fit For Purpose Leadership* then please contact *coachbiz@hotmail.com* and we will email you the *Writers Guide.*

# Did You Miss Past Editions Of
## *Fit For Purpose Leadership?*

The best-selling *Fit-For-Purpose Leadership series* is available on *Amazon* as both paperback and *Kindle*. In each edition, inspired leaders, worldwide, share their highest-value, current best thinking on business leadership.

# Join Leadership Gigs

Would you like to be a part of *Leadership Gigs?*

*Leadership Gigs* is a confidential forum for business leaders worldwide.

It operates as a closed *Whatsapp* and *Facebook* community. Our aim for this is to build a thriving community of business leaders who are helping each other's journey into the next decade.

One of the benefits is the opportunity to share your highest value thinking in the bestselling *Fit For Purpose Leadership* book series.

A good way to start to get involved is by requesting to join our *Facebook* group:

*http://bit.ly/LeadershipGigsFB*

Lightning Source UK Ltd.
Milton Keynes UK
UKHW020741290919
350673UK00015B/494/P